Letters from
Madelyn
Chronicles of a Caregiver

Distributed by Lainey Publishing
2725 Prominent Court South
Salem, OR 97302
Laineypublishing.com

Published by
Beautiful America Publishing Co.
P.O. Box 244
Woodburn, OR 97071

Library of Congress Catalog Number 2006038275

ISBN 0-89802-777-2

Printed in Korea

Letters from Madelyn

Chronicles of a Caregiver

by Elaine K. Sanchez

Dedication

To Madelyn –
my mentor, my friend, my mother.
Your light will forever shine.

Note to the Reader

Madelyn Kubin, my mother, lived on a farm six miles from town. She was the primary caregiver for my semi-invalid father, and she was losing her hearing. She felt isolated. She kept her sanity and maintained her connection to the outside world through writing letters, which were generally five to seven pages in length, typed, single-spaced, and often printed on both sides of the page. A favorite cousin once said, "When I get a letter from Madelyn, I make a pot of coffee, sit down, and plan to spend the morning with her."

She wrote extensively about my brothers and their families. She explored and expressed her feelings on faith, religion, politics, books, relationships, money, sex and anything else that came to mind. This book represents less than 10% of the content in the letters I received from her. I have edited heavily. There are some "holes" in the story that you will have to fill in for yourself. I simply couldn't tell it all.

In 1999, five and a half years after Quentin's stroke, Madelyn wrote, "I should have been keeping a journal all these years. It would be interesting now to see the stages I have gone through. It has taken many years to get to this place of detached peace and acceptance."

By publishing this book I want to honor her memory, share her insights and experiences, and fulfill her desire to help other people who may, at some time in their lives, have to face an incredibly difficult challenge.

Acknowledgement

I want to recognize the many "Friends of Madelyn" who read this book in its early stages. Special thanks to Tina Laologi who encouraged me move my mother from the pages of a novel into her own real story. Also, thanks to Barb Fromherz, Valerie Keever, Gerry Thompson, Lani O'Callahan, Caren Ann Jackson, Kathy Meier, Ellen and Charlie Weyent, Donna Armstrong, Father Lin Knight, Jinx Brandt and Jennifer Powers for taking the time to read and critique my early drafts. Their questions, thoughtful suggestions, and judicious use of red ink were invaluable.

I am grateful to Josh McMurrin for his inspired artwork and cover design; to Laurel Dryden for her unfailing patience and good humor when faced with endless edits, to Ted and Beverly Paul, my publishing gurus, for their guidance and sage advice.

And special thanks to my husband Alex, for recognizing and appreciating Madelyn's intelligence and humor; for providing love and support to both of us when we needed it most, and for encouraging me to tell her remarkable story of faith, love, and persistence.

Prologue

October 30, 1993

I picked up the ringing phone. It was my mother. "You're father's had a stroke."

"Oh, no!" A surge of panic rose in my chest. "How bad is it?"

"It's bad. It's affected his right side. He can't do much with his right hand; he's having trouble walking, and he can't talk right."

"What's the prognosis?"

"It's not good. The doctor says he has prostate cancer, too, and they think maybe the cancer's already spread to his brain."

"Oh, Mom," I said, sinking into the nearest chair. "I'm so sorry. What can I do?"

Her voice broke. "Can you come home?"

"Of course; I'll get on the road first thing in the morning."

The timing couldn't have been worse, but I couldn't say no, even though it meant missing my daughter's fifteenth birthday. I was also going to miss the high school football game Friday night. All season I had looked forward to walking out on the field on Moms' night with my oldest son Eric, a high school senior. He would give me a rose and a hug in front of the crowd. I wanted to cry when I thought of him walking out alone. It was a one-time experience that could never be recreated. People would feel sad for him and they would wonder about his mother.

I left Colorado Springs early the next morning. As I drove the 450 miles across the vast, barren plains of eastern Colorado and western Kansas, my mind refused to grasp the idea that my dad, a healthy, robust man could be brought down by a stroke.

He was still farming. He and Mom were going to Florida after Christmas where they had a condo rented for ten weeks. Dad would play golf every day with my Uncle Frank. They would laugh, drink beer, and joke with friends. Mom would read, attend classes at Unity and spend time with her sister Jean. At night they would visit and go out for dinner.

Dad was only 75. People in our family didn't get sick or die in their seventies. When Uncle John bought a new suit on his 93rd birthday he got two pairs of trousers to make sure the pants didn't wear out before the jacket. Dad was supposed to have another twenty years, at least.

It just wasn't right!

But then, a lot of things weren't right in my life, either. I was 42. I was divorced with three teenaged kids. My ex-husband hadn't held a steady job for a long time, and he didn't pay child support. I was still reeling from the loss of my job six weeks earlier as general sales manager for the NBC television affiliate in Colorado Springs, Colorado.

When my boss fired me I was four days away from closing on the sale of my 4,500 square foot home on a golf course and moving into a new, smaller town home. I was also driving a company car. In less than five minutes he told me he didn't like me anymore. He said I pushed myself and my employees too hard, that people were afraid of me, and I had to leave. In that brief and brutal span of time, I not only lost my job, I also lost my home and my car.

My confidence was deeply shaken. My future was uncertain; my children, who were also unsettled, upset, and confused, were pushing every limit, and my dad was dying. Naively, I thought things couldn't get any worse.

After eight hours on the road I finally reached McPherson, a small, flat town in central Kansas. I drove straight to the hospital. I was told to go to Rehab. I entered the room and was stunned when I realized the tiny, shriveled man being supported by the physical therapist on a slow-moving treadmill was my dad. He was wearing tennis shoes and forest green sweats, bunched up and twisted at the waist. I'd never seen him in clothes like that. He looked at me and tried to smile. His mouth was lopsided and his brown eyes, normally twinkling with mischief and laughter, were abnormally round and wide. He looked scared and helpless – like an animal caught in a trap.

I looked at my mother, who had just turned 70 and wondered how she was going to manage what lay ahead. A cottony puff of thin, white hair scarcely concealed her shiny, pink scalp. She still suffered with complications from the open-heart surgery she'd had four years earlier. Her back was humped from osteoporosis; her hearing was failing, and her eyes, always tired and aching from macular degeneration, drooped with fatigue and pain.

In addition to her physical limitations, she had very little money. Their only significant asset was 320 acres of land, half of which was homesteaded farm ground that had been in Dad's family since the late 1800's. There was no long-term-care insurance and only a few thousand dollars in savings.

I don't remember how long I stayed in McPherson. It couldn't have been more than three or four days. I did whatever I could to help Mom and encourage Dad, and then I had to go back to Colorado to rebuild my own shattered life. In the first few weeks after I lost my job I'd been forced to make a lot of quick decisions, including finding a place to live, buying a car, landing a job and taking the next step with a man in our relatively new relationship. Some of my decisions were good – a lot were not.

I was operating in a fog of confusion and self-doubt. I didn't understand why my life had unraveled so completely, and I wasn't sure I'd ever be able to piece it back together; but at least I still had choices.

Mom did not. Dad's stroke ended her freedom. There were days when she could escape for a few hours to run errands or attend a meeting, but for the most part she was held captive for the next six years on a Kansas farm six miles from a town of 10,000 people. And yet she never gave up looking for a positive perspective.

Her attitude toward life was nothing new. As a child I'd spent many hours sitting in the pit of the milk barn listening to her discuss the latest idea she had gleaned from a self-help or spiritual book. While she cranked grain into the metal stanchions, washed the manure off the cows' teats and swatted at flies, she would tell me about the latest thing she'd read. She loved books by Napoleon Hill and Norman Vincent Peale.

She told me over and over again, "You can be anything you want to be. You can do anything you want to do." She drilled into me the belief that every experience, good or bad, was an opportunity for personal and spiritual growth.

As Madelyn became a fulltime caregiver, her optimism and faith in a loving and benevolent God were tested daily. And when her physical and emotional capacities were stretched to the limit, she practiced the philosophy expressed by Viktor Frankl, a survivor of a Nazi concentration camp, in his book *Man's Search for Meaning*. Like Frankl, Madelyn accepted the fact that she could not control her circumstances, so time after time she acknowledged her situation and chose to change her attitude toward it.

1992, McPherson, KS–
Madelyn and Quentin's 50th anniversary

Madelyn's Family in 1993

Husband
Quentin
Married September 6, 1942.

Tacoma, WA–
Madelyn & Quentin's
wedding day

Children
Larry, born in 1946 - Married to Teri: Daughters Christy and Candi. Larry farms with Quentin and he and Teri live in the house next door.
Candi, Larry's youngest daughter and her family also live next door.

Greg, born in 1948, married to Deb: Children Mardee and John.
Owns an aerial spraying business in Moscow, Kansas.

Gene, married to Gloria: Children Jennifer and Danny.
Kansas City, KS

Elaine, divorced from Craig: Children Eric, Robert and Annie.
Colorado Springs, CO

Sister
Jean, married to Frank.
Hudson, Florida

Sister-in-law
Marg, widow of Dale – Quentin's brother
McPherson, KS

Chapter 1

January 6, 1994

Dear Elaine,

You will be glad to know that my chest pains have stopped. They got pretty bad right after Quentin had the stroke. I was beginning to wonder if I should go to the doctor, but I didn't want Quentin to know how much trouble I was having because he worries about the extra load I'm carrying.

One night I was reading an old Daily Word and I found the affirmation, "God is healing all now. Thank you, God." That really appealed to me. I started repeating it to myself over and over and my pains stopped.

Day before yesterday I couldn't stop crying. The last two months just came to a head. I'd had some chest pains during the day and a few in the night, but they have gone away again. It is such a relief to be free from them. I do indeed "Thank God."

It was a year ago today that we left for Florida. Kansas was covered with ice that night. It is supposed to get real cold here tonight – and I believe the weather forecasters are right – at 4:00 p.m. it was 25 degrees. We haven't been out of the house all day.

Quentin's still feeling sad about his brother. He said he didn't want to go over to the house right after Dale died because he thought I would be too upset. I finally said that I just had to go. We got over to Marg's house and Quentin cried real hard. He was real embarrassed that he cried; but it was all right, it endeared him to Marg. He was afraid to go to the funeral. He got through it okay, but he looked pretty tough. It was a beautiful service. There were lots of flowers and there were even people in the balcony.

The house you rented sounds dreadful, and it must be hard for the kids since they've always lived in a beautiful home, but I'm sure you won't have to stay there too long. I'm real proud of you for what you are doing. So many people blame everyone else for their troubles and problems and they never go to the effort to look within to see what needs to be changed. You will come out of this stronger, smarter, and more compassionate rather than bitter and defeated.

The new job sounds interesting. Have to admit I don't know much about the corporate hospitality business. I can't imagine how you'll convince companies to spend so much money on taking employees or clients to baseball games, but I never understood how you got people to spend so much on television advertising, either. If the Rockies turn out to be as popular as the Broncos, you should do real well. And even though the commute to Denver makes your days awfully long, it's good that you're taking the time to think about the things you need to do to change your life.

I've been thinking about your kids a lot and I think the dilemma is very predictable. They don't like having to share you with someone else, and I wouldn't be surprised if they don't resent someone else taking "Daddy's" place. It must be very hard for them to get used to John living in your house. You are raising kids in a very difficult time and they are a very difficult age. I don't envy you, and I pray for all of you every night.

We are looking forward to seeing you again, but don't come until your situation is under control. Quentin is still having so much trouble breathing and the flu or a virus would devastate him.

He still gets nervous very easy, but is doing better. He doesn't like to have me talk about his sickness, or anyone else's for that matter. That's the reason I'm writing. So when you do come home we can spend our time on much more interesting subjects. I get real lonesome to see people and to have a good conversation.

Love,

Mom

Footnote: Madelyn studied and practiced the faith of Unity, and she refers to it frequently in her letters. Unity is a spiritual healing movement based in Lee's Summit, MO. It has close ties to Christian Science and New Thought. It teaches the principles of Christ, and the belief that salvation is available to all. Unity prints and distributes numerous publications focusing on the healing of body, mind, and spirit through prayer and right thinking.

February 3, 1994

Dear Elaine,

On Tuesday we celebrated our 54th anniversary of having met each other. We went to Salina for lunch. Quentin had a petite steak and a small dish of ice cream. He's not supposed to eat much beef. He is also not supposed to have ice cream. It was terribly cold and windy. Since then he hasn't been as good. I think he got too tired.

We also went to the medical doctor on Tuesday and he prescribed a sleeping pill that he said was not addictive. It's helped. The muscles on Quentin's right side start jumping and wake him up. The doctor said that was common with stroke patients. Last night he took the sleeping pill and went right to sleep. He started jumping, but it didn't wake him up. I got jumpy myself and got up, as I could not sleep with all of his movement.

We went to the Chinese acupuncturist on Monday. She warned him about things to do to avoid having another stroke. The thought of another stroke really bothered him. That night he was having trouble handling everything and he got real agitated.

I finally said, "You can't let anything happen to you now. Elaine has all she can handle without you getting sicker or dying. She can't take one more thing." He's actually been improving every day since then.

Guess I don't need to tell you again how sorry I am about the way things have gone for you. Hope it will eventually turn out to be a blessing for everyone. Sometimes these rough times are turning points that become a real blessing. I can't help but feel that it won't take the kids long to get a perspective on things.

Have to run. You know we love you and are praying for you and yours.

Lots of love,

Mom

February 6, 1994

Dear Elaine,

I feel so "blah" today. I have written to my sister Jean and that's just about my total accomplishment, except for making the beds, fixing three meals and washing a load of clothes. I did help Quentin with his shower this morning. Yesterday I managed to get the magazine racks and refrigerator cleaned and felt good about the day.

I went to a home in McPherson that had a sign in front saying Kirby supplies were available. I was desperate for dirt bags, so we went there. I have never in my life seen such a mess. I went out to the car and told your dad that I had seen someone who was messier than me. It didn't comfort me – it scared me. Decided I had better get everything straightened out and develop some habits that will be helpful as I get older. Can't believe I need to clean my closet again. I did it only six years ago!

I will sure be glad when it warms up so we can get out and walk. Quentin isn't walking nearly as well as he did for a while. He has had some trouble with his rear end, so he doesn't feel like riding the bicycle. He was all broken out and has had trouble sleeping because of his itching skin. We think the chlorine in the swimming pool caused the irritation. We haven't been to the Y since the first of December, but his skin is just about healed now.

It's harder all the time for him to get out of bed. Thank goodness Greg came home and installed the ceiling hoist. I honestly don't know what we would do if we didn't have it. Last week I happened to be in the bedroom several times when Quentin was struggling, and I helped him up with the hoist. Then one night, I had severe chest pains. It used to never scare me, but it's hard to not get real concerned now, as I am needed very much. I sat in a chair and worked at relaxing. I have a little ball with knobs on it that is great for using reflexology on hands. I had read that rubbing the end of the little finger on the left hand has stopped lots of chest pains, so I did that and I put on a nitro patch. The pains didn't last too long, but I did learn that I just can't be pulling him up all the time.

When he is tired at night he breathes as if he's run up about three flights of stairs. I asked one time if the trouble came from his head or his chest. He said it was his chest. I asked where it hurt, and he said it went deep. He asked me one time to pray that he would die from heart trouble. I can't bring myself to do that, but I hope when the time comes for him to make his transition that it will be fast. I'm so glad he's not in pain. He has some discomfort at times, but he is not in terrible pain.

Sometimes I feel like I'm toilet training a little child. I'm always either asking if he needs to use the bathroom or I'm telling him to do so. Sometimes when he goes to lie down for a nap during the daytime, he won't use the bathroom. In just a little bit he'll need to go, but he can't get up in time. So now every time he goes to lie down I tell him to go to the bathroom first. When he says he doesn't need to, I tell him to go anyhow. When we go to town we take the urinal along, as he quite often has to go and there isn't a bathroom. He has a lot better control now that I've been questioning him about every two hours. I have to be careful that I don't show irritation with him.

The one place where I don't give in to him is when I want to sit up and read at night. He never wanted me to do that when he was well. Now he says he can't sleep if the light is on and the noise of the turning pages bothers him. He never has any trouble sleeping in the daytime. The dishwasher can be going, the TV can be on and the sweeper running and he can sleep without any problem. I told him last night to not worry if he couldn't sleep while I was reading, because he wouldn't have any trouble when it's daytime and I'm working. I need some time for myself and if he can't sleep, he will just have to stay awake.

It is not a fun-filled life for either one of us. Fortunately, there are still a lot of things I can do. He can only read, sleep or watch TV.

I enjoyed talking to Eric the other night. He said his dad hopes to move them out of Grandma Jane's basement and into their own apartment soon. Even though she loves them all, I can't imagine she's enjoying having Craig and your three kids living with her. I know I wouldn't want them!

I think Eric can do very well as a waiter if he doesn't get too unhappy with his customers. If he makes enough money, he'll probably learn to be patient. I know a young woman in Chicago who is working as a waitress. She got a degree in sociology but couldn't get a job in that field. She's doing real well financially. Her mother said she likes to wait on Jews and homosexuals, as they tip very generously.

I have enclosed the letter I sent to Eric in his birthday card. I hope he will take the time to read it and think about it.

Lots of love,

Mom

January 30, 1994

Dear Eric,

As I think back 18 years to the day you were born, the tears are streaming down my face. I have told you before how happy and proud everyone was. I hope we can all feel that way again soon. I hope you will read this letter all the way through. If you can't now, please save it and read it another time.

As I told you yesterday, I am so sorry about what has happened. It is up to you now to shape your life the way you want it to be. You are old enough to be considered a man, so you are old enough to make your decisions as to how you are going to live. I had a friend who told her kids, "Don't blame me for your life. I've done the best I know how. If you are smart enough to know what is wrong, you are smart enough to correct it."

Every day of our lives we make decisions that have an influence on the following days. Some decisions are not momentous ones—others are. The decisions to drink, do drugs, get involved in crime, etc. frequently have devastating effects that are painful to correct.

I keep thinking about where you are going live since you can't abide by your mother's rules. I doubt very much that your friend's parents would be thrilled to have another disagreeable, slovenly teenager around. If you stay with a friend, you had better hang up your coat, keep your room clean, get to meals on time, stay out of trouble, be agreeable, and pay some rent.

As I told you yesterday, I am trying to think of your good qualities and envision you using them. I was so proud of you the summer you worked at Village Inn and you took pride in being the best dishwasher that restaurant ever had. It is admirable to be a good dishwasher at sixteen, but it loses a lot when a person is an adult and can't do anything else. You will find that your chances for a good job are very slim without college.

Until recently you have been kind, loving and supportive of your mother, which was another admirable trait. Whatever you do, don't base your actions on trying to hurt her because it won't work. She has been hurt about as much as she can be, and anything you do to hurt her further will hurt you even worse.

You and your mother are very angry with each other now and I am hoping that in time you will remember all the loving things she has done for you and how she was always there loving and supporting you.

I hope you are still reading and that you will keep in touch with me. Remember, I have confidence that you have the ability to succeed. You must graduate from high school and you must decide on the future. It is all in your hands. You can watch the interviews on TV with the homeless people and decide if that is the way you want to live. You have always lived in a beautiful home and had good clothes. No one else is responsible for seeing that you continue that way except you.

As I said before, we all make our choices and then we have to live with them. Your Uncle Gene made some bad choices. We had co-signed a note for him at the bank and he was about to default on his loan. He was so worried that we were going to lose our farm because of his debt that he chose to fly Marijuana in from Mexico. He ended up spending time in prison. Turned out to be the best thing that could have happened to him, but it sure was a painful lesson for him, not to mention his wife and Grandpa and me (to name a few).

I have said a lot of times that I prayed him into prison because he was going wrong and that was the only thing that changed him. I didn't pray for him to go to prison, but that's what it took to get him straightened out. He is extremely smart, but cannot get a good job because of his record and not having a college degree. He could probably do a lot of jobs better than most college graduates, but he can't get a chance.

We have been praying for all of you every night that you will accept God's guidance and love in your lives. We will continue. However, God will not come down and hit you on the head with a good job, life or opportunity.

He can only do for you what he can do through you.

You have the mind and the ability to do something challenging and worthwhile—now do it!

God bless and love,

Grandma

May 15, 1994

Dear Elaine,

Teri mentioned last week that she thought Quentin should be in an intensive rehabilitation program. I called the doctor and he said we should call the rehab center at Wesley Hospital in Wichita. I got a hold of some idiot on the phone and she said, "You would drive all the way down here?" She went on to say that she doubted if they could get him in and recommended I contact the rehab hospital on the west side of town. I kept calling different places, and it seemed to me that everyone I talked to was so dumb and unknowledgeable that they wouldn't be able to help him anyway.

I finally got in touch with a delightful woman who is going to come to the house on Monday to evaluate him. Her company offers speech, physical, and occupational therapy. We are looking forward to having her come and hearing what she has to say. I spent a fortune on the telephone (during prime time) trying to find something. I talked to a woman who used to go to our church who is now a speech therapist in Hutchinson. She wasn't very encouraging, as she said there was a time limit for Medicare following a stroke. She said it could be terribly expensive now.

Still, I'm going to pursue it. Sometimes I can't understand a word he says. He has to repeat himself about three times for me to catch enough to figure out what he is saying. He blames it on my hearing, but it is still demoralizing for him and I feel bad about it. I miss not being able to talk to him, and I want my buddy back.

We had a tragic and shocking event in town last week. Delbert and Mildred Peterson were found dead. He was in his pajamas in the living room and she was in the garage in a car. The pickup and car had both been running, and apparently the door between the garage and the house was open because there was carbon monoxide in the house and the dog was dead, too. I think it must have been twenty years ago that Delbert told Quentin if anything happened to him (Quentin) that I'd be able to handle it. He went on to say that his wife wasn't that strong. In the last four years she's had two strokes, two mastectomies, both knees replaced, etc., etc. She had an appointment to go to an oncologist on Friday. No one knows exactly what happened or why, but there are about as many stories as there are people to tell them.

I can understand their desperation, but I don't think I could ever accept suicide as a solution.

Have to run to get this in the mail.

Love,

Mom

May 18, 1994

Dear Elaine,

I'm so happy you got moved into your new house. It sounds wonderful. I know it was hard on you living in the "ghetto" rental house. Women's rights have come a long way. It wasn't long ago that a single woman would have had a hard time buying her own home.

I looked at the Rockies schedule this evening and see that they have a lot of home games for the next two weeks, so it looks as if it will be hard to call you. I hope all your parties go well. I can't imagine that GM would spend $10,000 for one party at a baseball game. I'm happy for you, but I bet they could sell their cars for a lot less if they weren't quite so free with their money.

I went in for blood tests earlier in the week. The LPN stuck me three times before she gave up and called for help. When the nurse came in I told her I hoped the doctor would get busy enough that the LPN would get practiced in taking the blood.

The doctor called today to say everything was fine except the triglycerides. It should be under 200 and mine was 480. We've been eating eggs every morning and have had a lot of toast with Parmesan cheese. I told Quentin I thought we might be eating too many eggs.

He said, "Don't take my eggs away. What am I going to eat?"

I was standing by a window looking out at the grass, and I told him I was thinking about putting him out to eat grass. Guess I will have to go with him.

Your dad seems to be doing better. He played golf with Gene on both Saturday and Sunday. When he got tired he just rode along in the cart. He doesn't hit the ball a long distance, but it seems to be going pretty straight.

He's been doing a little bit of tractor work. He planted corn for a couple hours last Friday – worked in the field a couple hours yesterday morning and then mowed the lawn for four hours. He is still having trouble with his breathing and the phlegm in his throat, but it is better. He has not made the divan out into a bed for over a week now. We both alternate between the La-Z-Boys, the couch and the bed, but he is getting more sleep than he did.

I sure felt good after seeing your kids the other day. They have a nice apartment with their dad. It's a duplex and is quite new. It was rather sparsely furnished and the furniture wasn't new, but it wasn't disreputable either.

The boys said I couldn't go downstairs – that was their area and it was terrible. Eric is looking forward to going to college in the fall. They all seemed to be in good shape. I told Eric when you were coming for his graduation and said I hoped you could get together. He said, "We'll see." He had tears in his eyes, so I thought that was encouraging.

Your relationship with your kids right now is not as unusual as one might think. I have heard of several situations of estrangement that did eventually get straightened out. The training the kids have had from you is a real asset to them now. They do know how to take care of themselves—cook, clean, do laundry, etc.

I think I told you about getting up one morning and having this thought come through: "They are nourished from the roots." I don't know for sure what that means, but I felt very peaceful about it. I would guess they all realize you weren't responsible for them acting the way they did and realize that you had reason to be very angry. I'm sure their dad keeps feeding them a lot of his anger, which makes it difficult for them.

I'm sorry John is giving you a hard time about coming back for Eric's graduation. I can see why he doesn't think much of your kids right now, but I do agree with you that this is important. Graduation is something that only happens once. I admire you for sticking to your guns.

Even if they won't admit it right now, your kids love you and they need to know that you still love them. Besides, I'm sure John's daughter will enjoy having some one-on-one time with him. I wonder if she'll want to move to the U.S. too. England might look old and dreary in comparison to Colorado.

Everything here is so lush right now. Quentin and Teri mowed the yard Tuesday and it's beautiful. I am enjoying the tree you gave me. I planted my flowers from seed this year. It's cheaper and there is a fascination to watching the plants come up and grow. I have ten tomatoes, two peppers and one zucchini plant. Have to transplant some more flowers tonight.

Lots of love,

Mom

June 23, 1994

Dear Elaine,

Quentin and I were taking a nap the other day and he heard the word, "FIRE!" on our business band radio. The temperature was close to 100, but thankfully the wind wasn't blowing. The fire started inside one of the combines. Gene saw it and yelled on the radio to Candi that she had a fire. She grabbed her water jug and the fire extinguisher and jumped off the platform, but the stubble had already caught fire. Larry came on the scene at that time and he called to everyone to get their equipment out of the field.

When Quentin finally got his pants on he stood up and said, "I can't take this."

My heart started pounding real hard and I said, "I can't take it either," but we couldn't stay home, so we both went.

We decided to take the van in case we needed to haul people to the hospital. On the way over to the fire Quentin told me to take him by the field where he'd been working earlier so he could get the tractor and plow.

I called 911 and gave the fire department directions to the field, but as Quentin and I were driving I commented they wouldn't have any trouble finding it as there was a big, long line of smoke. There were two real dark spots, and Quentin thought it looked like equipment burning.

When I got to the field Teri's folks were already there. They'd seen the smoke on their way home from town. I was relieved when I got there and found out everyone was alright. I told them that Quentin was on his way over with a tractor. We all looked down the road and here he was coming. It was a very dramatic, memorable moment – there wasn't another vehicle in sight – just this one John Deere with Quentin driving it. There was absolute silence for a few seconds, and then Teri and her mother started saying that Quentin shouldn't be out in the smoke, which was quite intense.

Larry went buzzing out of the field in his pickup, met Quentin at the corner and they traded. As I mentioned earlier, it was hotter than hell and all the kids were about prostrate. All the water had been used to stop the fire.

Teri's mother, sister and I went to the house and grabbed everything we thought might be helpful. I took a sack of ice, several bottles of drinking water, two big pitchers of orange juice, a carton of Pepsi, three wet towels and lots of cups. We had plenty for everyone – even the firemen. An ambulance came out from town.

When the fire was out and everyone had been refreshed, Larry commented that he needed to get his combine out of the field. Quentin volunteered to go get it. Larry let him open up the adjoining field – I guess to see if the combine was working all right. When Quentin got off, he said he knew he couldn't drive a combine anymore, but he had sure enjoyed that. He hadn't been so happy in ages.

Quentin went back to the field to continue plowing. When he came in at 6:30 for supper I said, "You aren't going back to the field, are you?"

He said there was just a little bit left in the field and he wanted to finish it. At 8:00 I called him on the radio and asked if he was going to work all night (in a not-too-nice tone of voice). He assured me that he was almost through. He finally came dragging in at 9:30.

I'm not at all proud of myself, but I met him at the back door hollering, "If you have another stroke it had better by-God kill you!"

I went flouncing off to the living room. He came in and said he was sorry- he just hadn't realized how late it was. I was still mad and informed him that you didn't have to be particularly smart to know when you watched the sun go down, dark settle in and the moon start to shine that it was time to quit. He had been out since 7:30 in the morning with just a little over an hour off at noon and time enough to grab a quick sandwich in the evening.

I'm still convinced the reason he had the stroke was because he'd been working too hard. When he said he was retiring last year, he promised he wouldn't work on Sundays or after supper any more, but he still came in every night between 9:00 and 11:00 pm.

I feel I was entitled to be scared and mad, but he did look so good and happy that I'm sorry I jumped on him the way I did. He hasn't had much energy since. Who knows whether it's because he worked too long and got too tired, or because he was reminded so forcibly that he can't work and live the way he has for the last 48 years.

Love,

Mom

August 14, 1994

Sleeping in one bed has become almost impossible for us. We've spent most of our nights in our La-Z-Boys. It's easier for Quentin to breathe with his head elevated, and it seems to ease my back and chest pains.

I decided to buy two twin-sized hospital-type beds that we can scoot together. We can elevate the heads, and they bend around the knees, too. This will eliminate the problem of lying flat and we can still be together. I sincerely hope we like the new beds as much as we think we are going to. I know we would both feel much better if we could go to bed and sleep all night.

I think we are going to get cable tomorrow. I don't need TV because I can't hear and I really prefer to read, but reading is hard for Quentin now. He just can't concentrate, but he can enjoy TV. Won't it be wonderful that we'll be able to watch the O.J. Simpson trial from beginning to end – all day!! I can hardly wait!

There are so many things we can't do or don't want to do, that we've decided we'd better make life as pleasant and comfortable as we can. We are so grateful for the trips we've taken and the fun we've had. We might never be able to do a lot of those things again, but there's no point in sitting around crying over what can't be. We need to concentrate on what is possible and what we can enjoy. We don't enjoy eating out much any more. It almost makes me ill when the bill comes.

I met my friend Vera in town yesterday. She got a dish of ice cream and I ordered a piece of blueberry pie. It was absolutely awful. I was eleven years old when I made my first pie, and I had a much better crust. The crust on this one was about as thick as a cookie and not nearly as good. When the bill came it was $1.75 for that lousy piece of pie!

Love,

Mom

September 27, 1994

Dear Elaine,

I'm sorry about the baseball strike. I know you've worked real hard on your hospitality business and the concession stands. Damn ball players! I don't suppose they ever once thought about how many people they'd put out of business with their stupid strike.

So far I haven't written a list of your accomplishments and abilities and why someone should be delighted to have you with their company, but I keep going over it mentally. I'm sure there are hundreds of companies that would benefit immensely from having you on their payroll and would feel it was their lucky day when you came along. Just keep faith and keep believing the doors are going to open. Hope you enjoy the Daily Word and

Unity magazine as much as I have. The article on Transitions in the magazine is especially applicable for you.

I've been thinking about you and John a lot, and I think it's just as well that he is going back to England. I thought it was pretty narrow-minded of him to say he wouldn't ever be able to forgive your kids. But he was absolutely right when he said you wouldn't be able to love him if he kept you away from them. There is nothing more powerful than a mother's love, and he's smart to know that.

He was a very wonderful part of your life at just the right time and you have enjoyed a beautiful friendship. You have lots of great memories that will always be a part of your life. I know you're feeling sad. It's always hard to be disappointed in someone you care about. Still, I'm hoping that with him out of the picture your kids might feel differently. I don't think they liked him any more than he liked them.

I forgot to tell you the other night that Robert was elected president of DECCA and he feels real good about that. Annie said it was a real honor. When I talked to him on the phone, he told me about it. Will try to get back with Annie this week and see if things are better for her. I think she's really missing you. I'm glad you are continuing to send letters to the kids. Even if they don't respond they're still getting the message that you care.

Lots of love,

Mom

Chapter 2 - 1995

January 6, 1995

Dear Elaine,

I'm glad you didn't have any trouble with the weather going back to Colorado Springs. I'm so happy you were here for Christmas. It was good to be with you and the kids again. I know you had worried about not being able to spend as much money on gifts as you had in the past, but I think the photo albums you made for each of them were more meaningful than any store-bought present could have ever been.

I was struck by the number of pictures of all of the cakes you had decorated for their birthdays, all the homemade Halloween costumes and the big Christmas celebrations you had each year. They can't look at those albums without remembering what a great mom you were when they were little. I thought they all got a little teary-eyed when they were looking at their pictures, even though they laughed a lot. Anyway, it turned out to be a good Christmas, and we were happy to be with all of you again.

I'm sorry you hate your job. I know selling grocery store billboards is a big step down from being the general sales manager of an NBC television affiliate. Still, it's better to have a damaged ego than a stack of unpaid bills. I'm sure something better will come along soon.

It was two years ago today we left for Florida. It seems like a decade. I commented to Quentin last night that he needed to read a little bit to sharpen up his brain. I brought home a book from the library recently. He said it was probably good, but he'd read the first chapter twice and the second one three times trying to get the characters straight. He finally just gave up.

I told him that if he doesn't challenge his mind he will get worse. I explained how new dendrites grow to replace the part of the brain that's dead. He said he's keeping his mind active by talking to Larry about fertilizer, herbicide, marketing, etc. I know that's a help, and I am so grateful he has that opportunity. We would both just die (maybe shoot ourselves) if he had no outlet.

It's cold and windy, so I'm going to drive to the mailbox. Want to get there before the mailman comes.

Love,

Mom

February 8, 1995

Dear Elaine,

As I was preparing breakfast this morning I suddenly remembered what I wanted to talk to you about. Have a lot that I should be doing – like breakfast dishes and folding clothes – but I want to talk.

I've thought about the counselor asking if you felt

like you were going back to second place. I am very disturbed with the advice that is being given to people about "doing your own thing and to hell with everyone else." I think that is responsible for a lot of the divorces and unhappiness in the world today.

Dr. Wayne Dwyer had a lot to do with this when he wrote the book, *Your Erroneous Zones.* I bought the book and it made me so angry I couldn't finish reading it. Same with the book *Dance of Anger.* I get very angry and up on my high horse when I think about that one, too. For one thing, I had the feeling Dwyer didn't realize there were two genders. In my opinion he was only aware of the male. For another, he kept pounding at the idea that you should do what you want to do.

As an old lady, I'm here to tell anyone who will listen that life is not made of up of doing what you want to do! When a person commits to marriage and parenthood, your time of living for yourself is gone – FOREVER!

When I look back over my life, it is hard to see what I have done just for myself. I have, of course, learned to find my own space and time in my mind. Finding Unity has been the greatest thing that ever happened to me. I have said for many years that living strictly on the physical plane has very little joy for me. I can't see why some people fight so hard to live.

I can't see anything so wonderfully exciting or invigorating about getting up in the morning, fixing breakfast, doing dishes, making the bed, picking up the papers, doing laundry, fixing lunch, doing dishes, doing some more laundry and housework. An exciting day for me might include a good telephone conversation, or possibly meeting an interesting person in the grocery store or on the street. And for this I should spend money on vitamins, try to eat right and exercise so I can prolong this wonderful life experience? HA!

The joy I have comes from sharing with Quentin (and that does not usually include doing just what I want to do). As a matter of fact, I have felt very restricted in doing what I want to do, and it is much more so now. You are a big joy to me, and I cannot imagine my life without you. There are many things, but one of the big joys is being able to share thoughts with you. There is no one else I can be so free with. I do love the boys, but the relationship is so very different.

Getting along with daughters-in-law does not always come under the title of "doing just what I want to do." I love and enjoy the grandkids too – there again there is very little that qualifies as "doing what I want to do." There are none of these relationships, including the one with you, where I can say I am number one and I can and will only do what I want to do within that relationship.

My greatest joy in life comes from learning and

growing mentally and spiritually. The great thing about having your "space and happiness from within" is that a person can stay more or less detached and still do what has to be done to give other people a reasonable amount of happiness.

Well, I could probably write a book on this, but Quentin will be in for lunch before long, so I'd better get on with it.

Lots of love,

Mom

February 9,

I'm going to try to finish this letter now. Quentin had a good appointment with the dentist yesterday. Good to have something go right. He and Larry were discussing plans for the summer crops and Quentin seemed so alive and happy this evening. It made me think of how much fun he used to be.

I'm glad Annie is coming back to live with you. If your boys can't bring her, we could pack her things in our pickup. I can't say I'd look forward to having the three of us in the cab and the (damned) dog. When we were both so sleepy at noon, Quentin asked how we would make the eight hour trip. I told him we might have to rent a motel room for a couple hours. He suggested that we could let Annie drive. We'll see.

Love,

Mom

February 21,

Dear Elaine,

Thank you for the wonderful Valentine card. I still have it on the little table on my lamp stand and I read it every day. I don't know where you get such beautiful cards. We appreciated the pictures, too.

I had made an appointment to see an ear doctor in Hutchinson today. I got a call this morning saying he had been called to court. I had to change my appointment to Friday. I was tempted to ask if he was involved in a malpractice suit, but I didn't. I had already called Annie and made arrangements to see her, so I went to Hutchinson anyhow.

I went to their apartment around 3:30. I rang the doorbell and Craig answered. He said Annie wasn't home from school yet. They have to be out of their apartment by February 28. He plans to leave the same day for his new job in Oklahoma. I asked him if the boys had found a place to live yet, and he said they hadn't. He said they would just have to look out for themselves. I was very helpful and said, "Well, I guess they could always sleep in their cars." There wasn't much to say after that.

He told me I could wait inside, but I would have felt uncomfortable, and it was such a nice day that I sat in the car. Eric came home while I was waiting for Annie. He was really shot. He had just gotten off work and he was so sleepy and tired he could hardly keep his eyes open. I gave him his belated birthday card. I had enclosed the article about the chef from McPherson who won the trip to France. I had underlined the sentence telling about how he'd started out washing dishes in McPherson. I also wrote the letter, which I am enclosing. I really didn't expect him to read it in my presence, and he didn't. He opened it and silently searched for a check (which wasn't there) and then he went inside to go to bed.

Annie and I had a few minutes to visit. She told me she was scared about moving back with you, and I told her you were scared too. I told her I was confident that it could work and that I certainly hoped so for both of you. I also told her I didn't think the problem would be getting along with you, but I was worried that she'd really miss Eric and Robert. She agreed with that.

She stated that going through the divorce and everything that had happened this past year had really brought them close. She said when they talked to other people about everything that happened they would say, "I know how you feel."

They realized no one else could know how it felt except for the three of them, so they've discussed everything between themselves. She said they didn't feel like talking about it to other people any more. She also said the boys are seriously thinking about coming to Colorado to go to college next year.

She sure is a pretty girl. I love her eyes. Christy said they are just like mine. The only similarity I see is that they're brown. Her eyes have such a fascinating shape. She almost looks exotic.

Quentin and I went and exercised at the Y this morning. We always come right home and go to bed as we are very tired. After lunch Quentin went out and drove a tractor for four-and-a-half hours. He is very tired this evening but happy. He is also riding the stationary bike. He is determined to make his legs stronger, and that is good.

Tomorrow morning we go to Salina to the urologist so Quentin can get another shot. We will stop at Sam's and pick up some things we need and then hurry home. We have our World Religion class at 1:00 o'clock. I told my sister about it and had to laugh when she wrote back and said, "That course is not my cup of tea. Your Mr. Smith would have to tell some dirty stories to keep me there for three hours."

It was very interesting last week, even though we did feel a little out of place with all the teachers, preachers and other people with college degrees. Thank goodness my friend Rene is there. She doesn't have a college degree either.

I'm sure getting a lot of mileage out of thinking about being Number One. I have said many times that the cows were number one – then baseball and then me. Quentin gave up baseball, so I moved up a space. Then farming was solidly in first place and I was second. When he got really involved in golf I nearly slipped into third place again.

Lots of love,

Mom

Dear Eric,

This is a delayed acknowledgment of your birthday. I have been thinking about you a lot. Understand you are very busy with your two jobs. I've enclosed an article from the McPherson paper which you might find interesting and inspirational. This man started out doing dishes at the Country Club. Couldn't help but think you two had some of the same qualities.

Annie told me that Robert would be in Overland Park in a DECCA contest. I gave her Jennifer and Danny's telephone number—hope he calls them. Jennifer has enlisted in the Marines and will leave on September 18. I get a sick feeling when I think about her going through boot camp, but she has confidence she can handle it.

She will make $900 a month while in boot camp and $1,500 when she finishes. That's pretty good when a person considers it includes room, board, clothes, medical, education, etc. She is very fluent in the Japanese language and would like to be stationed in Japan.

The service is sure different than when your grandpa was in. He started out at $21.00 a month. He did get in the Air Corps, which was his choice. In those days, they usually put you in the job for which you were least qualified and you had nothing to say about it. I know the standard for being in the service is much higher now, but I hadn't thought much about the pay. I can see that if they want high quality people they have to pay for them, which is okay by me.

Everything is dull and low key around here. Grandpa and I are going to a water exercise class twice a week. We have to set the alarm clock for 6:00 am in order to have our breakfast and leave here at 7:15. In January it was just like night when we went out. The moon was shining and there were two big stars visible. It was brutally cold most of the mornings – just miserably cold the rest of the time. We sure ought to get an "E" for effort for trying to improve our stamina and bodies.

There was an article in the paper a couple years ago telling about all of the college grants available that aren't used—six million dollars, in fact. I went to the library last week and asked for information about college grants and scholarships. The librarian brought me four books. I looked through them briefly then decided it was your job and not mine.

I have discontinued giving birthday money to the grandkids this year for a couple reasons. One is that money is very short here right now. Frankly, I suppose the real honest to goodness reason is that I have never had anyone acknowledge having received the money. The only way I know it has been received is when I see the cancelled check. I have debated a long time with myself whether to say anything or not, but decided I really should. I would guess there are others who feel the same way.

We wish you the very best for the coming year and always. We will be following your career with interest. Have you seen the ad on TV where they say, "A mind is such a terrible thing to waste"? You have a wonderful mind, good health and the world ahead of you. It is an enviable position to be in.

It isn't very exciting to be in the position we are now where you realize every time you buy something new that it will probably be the last time you make that kind of purchase. It's also frustrating to know there is no way you can get a job to add to your income and that you don't have the opportunity to make long-range plans any more.

We've had a good life and a good marriage, and there does seem to be a built-in clock that knows the whole show could be over any time. It's something a person seems to know and in a way accept. It is much easier for us than it would be for someone your age to know life will be over in a few years. When one has lived life well and has no regrets about choices or actions, there seems to be an in-born intelligence that realizes what is happening and accepts it without self-pity or fear.

Well, so much for that. Grandpa and I pray every night that our five older grandchildren will not do anything to harm their minds or bodies and that they will make the right choices at this very important time of their lives.

Lots of love,

Grandma

February 26, 1995

Dear Elaine,

We have enjoyed our World Religion class, but I did blow my front of being a sweet, little, old white-haired lady the other day. We were studying the many different religions in India and their customs. They are still killing baby girls over there. Someone did a survey fairly recently and came to the conclusion that they are one million women short. I refrained from making some unladylike remark about hoping the guys will have to start screwing themselves soon.

The custom of killing baby girls has been outlawed, but it's still done. Then there was the custom of burning a man's body when he died. A really good wife was supposed to go jump on top of the pyre and burn with the old goat. If she didn't, she was supposed to express terrible grief the rest of her life – she wasn't even supposed to comb her hair. The brothers-in-law were free to "use" her. It just went on and on like that, and of course, I was doing a slow burn.

I finally shocked them by saying that my favorite expression was the one about God creating man and then saying, "Oh, Hell. I can do better than that." And that's when he made woman.

I wasn't content to shut up there. I went on to say that God should have destroyed the first man and made another one. He'd had enough experience by then that He should have been able to come up with a reasonably good model.

One young man asked, "What does your husband think of that?" I said that he was used to my opinion and had heard it a lot of times.

I will be interested in seeing how they treat me this week. I nearly blew my top again, but they were talking low. One man said there are some who say the book of Solomon is an allegory and relates to Christ's relationship to the Church. I wanted to say it sounded like some damned men trying to put a good spin on that old sex pot. I'm going to try to read it again before the next class. I hope I can keep my cool and my ladylike ways and not tell them what I think about all those horny prophets in the Old Testament.

If I'm pushed I might also tell them if I were forced to choose between the God of the Old Testament and the Devil that I'd take the Devil every time. At least he was consistent!

Quentin and I both feel that this class has stimulated our thinking. I'm reading Deepak Chopra's books. He is an Indian. It is incredible to realize how much great wisdom has come out of India and how stupid they still are. Herb Smith said they were very advanced in math, science, medicine and many other things two thousand years before Jesus was born. This week we are going to study about Buddha. I really don't know much about him or the Buddhist religion, so that should be interesting.

Quentin and I were talking about your friend, the judge, and how he sounds so much like the other men you've had in your life. I think I've figured out why they're attracted to you. I told Quentin I think they see you as a challenge and they want to conquer you.

Quentin immediately replied, "No, that is not the reason. They think if they could conquer her, just look at what they would have."

They always show a good personality and a strength, which you admire. I can't remember a meek, weak man ever showing an interest in you, can you? Like I said, this was just a case of trying to figure out something, and anyway, we're glad you dumped him before you got too involved.

We were supposed to go back to the college this morning for our World Religion class, but Quentin didn't sleep very well, so he went back to bed. I told him to not worry about missing class and to sleep if he could. He is very concerned about his legs and his future. His legs have been bothering him for months. He's put off going to the doctor hoping the exercise class would strengthen them enough, but he realized last week it's not working.

We will see Dr. Kaufman tomorrow. He's the one who originally operated on Quentin's knees. He had to give up surgery, which he loved, because he's had a rough time with prostate cancer. I feel he will understand Quentin's situation. Your dad has had to give up so much already, but having to give up work is the hardest of all. He has it figured out that he's going to start the conversation by saying he can't do yard work, house work, play golf or dance and see what the doctor says. Later he will say that he can't do tractor work either. I think he's afraid if he starts out saying he can't do tractor work that the doctor will say, "So what?"

I know you can appreciate how we go back and forth in our thinking about knee replacement surgery. How about his breathing? How about the weakness in the right leg as a result of the stroke? In case he does have the surgery, it will probably be on both knees. I keep saying we will pray about it. Pray for the doctor to make the right decision and then wait. You can well imagine how hard it is to put it out of our minds.

We are grateful for Teri and Larry. One of them will go with us to this appointment. Teri has been good about not pushing her opinions on us, and she doesn't hover over us and act as if we are old people who can't take care of ourselves. We appreciate that too.

We thought about you a lot over the weekend and hoped all of you had a wonderful time. I will be eager to hear how Annie reacted to the big welcome. We are so glad you are having a chance to be mother and daughter again. We have prayed all of your children would remember all the love you had given them, what you had tried to teach them and that they would feel the same love they had before. Now, we feel like we can say, "Thank you, God." We will still be praying for guidance for all of you.

It is such a joy to us to know that you have a job you like and things are going well. We are proud of the way you have handled the last eighteen months. I never knew there were businesses that placed high tech employees in companies on a temporary basis. I wonder if selling people's skills will be a lot different from selling advertising. It sounds like you will have the opportunity to meet a lot of interesting people.

I always admire the way you look to yourself to find the problem. You don't waste time and energy in a negative way. As you know, when a person does that he/she not only has regrets about the past, but will soon have more regrets and lost opportunities.

Lots of love,

Mom

April 21, 1995

Dear Elaine,

I've been thinking about Robert all week. It's hard to believe he's 18 today. He was the sweetest baby and the cutest little boy I've ever known. He's had a rough couple years, but I think that sweetness is coming back. I stop in at Target to see him whenever I'm in Hutch. He says he's doing well in school. He and Eric seem to be getting along fine in their apartment.

I was so surprised when you said you've decided you need to move to Albuquerque. I expected you to say that you'd enjoyed your business trip, but I sure didn't expect to hear you say you intended to move there. However, I've learned over the years to trust my intuition, and I think you should trust yours. If you feel that strongly that you belong there, then you should go. I'll be eager to hear if your company will transfer you. It seems like you might be able to find more high-tech jobs for people in New Mexico because of Sandia and Los Alamos Labs. At any rate, we'll be interested to hear how it all develops.

I don't know if having the knee surgery was a mistake. Quentin doesn't have the intense pain any more, but he sure has lost ground in a lot of other ways.

I'll keep you posted.

Love,

Mom

July 7, 2005

Dear Elaine,

Congratulations on the new job and the move. It was good to talk to you last night. We do enjoy hearing about the various things you are experiencing. It is a bright spot in my life to know what is going on in yours. I don't mean to be snoopy – just living vicariously. It will be fun to learn about Albuquerque through your eyes.

I always forget to tell you how pretty my flowers are and how much I'm enjoying them. I really love the snap dragons. They are every color imaginable and most of them are two-colored. They just bloom and bloom. The flowers you planted in the flower boxes were getting ruined on the porch railing from all the rain. I moved them in front of the garage and they are doing really well. The wild flower garden is absolutely beautiful. There is something new starting to bloom all the time. Quentin has not been terribly impressed with them. I told him the flowers made me think of being in the mountains.

My tomatoes are a disaster this year. The hail was hard on them and I think they must have some kind of blight. I get so provoked. I'm very tempted to go out and chop them out and plant the ground to perennials, but my heart does not think hoeing is any fun at all. I want to have a lot of flowers next year that won't take a lot of work. I do enjoy getting out of the house and seeing the beauty of the flowers. It breaks the monotony of nothing but housework.

We went to our World Religion Class a few days ago. One of the young students challenged me to think of something good in the Old Testament. I was real proud of myself when I announced, "Well, I do admire the Jews for getting that trash published!" That's one of the fun things about being a white-haired, little old lady. You can say just about anything you want and get away with it.

Going back to Quentin – he used the urinal last night instead of staggering to the bathroom. He couldn't get out of bed by himself. I had to take his arm and help him get up. We had the walker and the urinal in the bedroom, so it worked fine. He did not get a Depend wet all night, and that made him feel good.

I'm still having trouble getting him to use his cane. So

many times he will pick it up and carry it. I tell him that will not do him a bit of good if he starts falling.

I hate to write such a dismal, unpleasant letter, but it is full of facts that I feel you would want to know – or at least that I want to discuss with you. We love you very much and you are a bright spot in our lives.

Love,

Mom

July 30, 1995

Dear Elaine,

It's nice that Univision is paying the rent on your apartment until the house in Colorado Springs sells. I enjoy thinking about you and Annie spending your evenings around the swimming pool. It must seem like a vacation to both of you.

I'm glad you're back in the television business. I don't think you would have ever fully recovered from being fired if you hadn't taken this job. I told a few friends that you were working for a Spanish language television station. They were so surprised that you could get a job like that when you don't speak Spanish. I told them you didn't have to speak Spanish, that you were hired to teach the Hispanic sales staff how to sell advertising to white people.

We were both excited about coming to see you, but I

don't think that's going to happen. I haven't cancelled our reservations as yet, but I'm pretty sure that I will. It seems to me that your dad is getting worse each day. Some days are better than others. We can't either one figure out what in the world is happening.

There's another problem that I thought about this morning. He has to wear a Depend undergarment to bed. He usually goes through three of them in a night. Most of the time he gets to the bathroom, but there are times when the bed is wet all the way down to the rubber sheet. I would hate for him to urinate all over your mattress and carpet.

When he gets up in the night he tries so hard to get to the bathroom. It's heartbreaking to see the way he stumbles around trying to walk. I have trouble getting him to use the cane, and I have insisted that he keep it by the bed and use it at night. The other night he went to the bathroom and left the cane by the bed. I took it to the bathroom, plopped it down in front of him and said, "Use this damned thing!"

I flounced off to bed. When he came in, I told him that I was not going to call Larry in the middle of the night to come pick him up off the floor. I told him I would take him a pillow and a blanket and he could spend the rest of the night on the floor.

He laughed and said, "You wouldn't be that mean would you?"

I replied, "Just try me!"

A lot of times when we go to the park, he picks the cane up and carries it. The doctor told him the other day that he could get hurt falling. He has fallen six times in the last ten days. The doctor said he should use the cane for balance. I think he's done a little better since the doctor scolded him.

Yesterday morning when we went to town he walked great, but he didn't do so well this morning. Dr. Larzalere said some people who have had a stroke never completely recover from the knee surgery.

I asked the doctor if he could prescribe an anti-depressant that would work. The doctor asked if Quentin had trouble sleeping, and when we told him that did, he prescribed Elivel. One of the side effects is a dry mouth. The good news is I feel like I can see a difference. You mentioned the other night that depression is sometimes caused by a chemical mix-up in the body. The reason your dad needs an anti-depressant is an emotional one.

He has not been using his mind at all, and I can see he isn't as sharp. I have been fussing with him about that. I looked at Lego's yesterday and they were so terribly expensive. I asked him if he would use them with his right hand if I bought them. I bought a small set last year that made into an airplane. He had fun doing it and got along fine – but he used his left hand.

I've told him he ought to watch more TV, read, or play solitaire – anything where he would be using his mind.

I asked him yesterday what he thinks about all the time he sits at the kitchen table not doing anything. He looked out to our "hill", which had just been plowed that day and said how much he enjoyed seeing that. He also said he thinks about the crops and the farm.

I checked out a book at the library that I had read and thought he might like. It was about some men on the Louis & Clark expedition. One afternoon I had laid down for a nap, and a very unusual noise woke me up. I jumped out of bed and rushed to the dining room where he was sobbing. I couldn't understand what he was telling me, but I looked at the book and saw he was in a place where the wife and husband had to separate, and there was the possibility that the husband might not return. That was the cause of the sobbing. I got a couple real life books yesterday and hope he can get interested in them.

Our wheat crop came to about $2,000 this year, which is really not adequate. The crop adjuster will be here this week to see about the hail damage to the corn. Ours was hit at a very bad stage. It really doesn't look too bad now. Larry said a lot will depend on how much stalk damage there was. If there is a lot, smut or some other problem could develop.

Everyone wants to know how I am doing, and I appreciate the concern. I get along fine when I can put Madelyn aside and be a channel for love and caring. When the ego of Madelyn takes over, it is terrible. I can feel very frightened and very sorry for Madelyn. It is a miserable feeling, which I try to eliminate as quickly as possible.

This is a lot like the War. I used to say I wished I knew when Quentin was going to be home so I could mark off the days. It is probably just as well that I don't know what the future holds now. This could go on for years, which in my opinion, is the very worst thing that could happen. I could let Quentin go very easily now. He is not happy and he really doesn't have anything very wonderful to look forward to.

Quentin is ready to go to bed. It isn't 9:30 yet, but I will go too. I was reading a book this afternoon and didn't take a nap. I was very displeased with him last night. I didn't go to bed when he did because I was very interested in a book I was reading. I can be completely transported to a different time and place with a good book. He came in about midnight wanting to know when I was going to come to bed. He hadn't been asleep yet.

He can get up in the morning, eat breakfast and go back to bed and sleep like he's dead. He doesn't hear the telephone. When the cleaning lady was here last week, I told her to go ahead and run the sweeper as it wouldn't bother him – and it didn't. At night I think the flutter of gossamer butterfly wings would awaken him.

Love,

Mom

August 21, 1995

Dear Elaine

I have just helped Quentin get to the bathroom. We made it on time – thank goodness. He gets the urge to go with this diarrhea and he doesn't have any control. I came home from town last Tuesday and he met me at the bedroom door and told me to not step on the towel that was by his chair in the dining room. There was a big pile of shit on it. He had gotten his clothes off and taken a shower but got the urge while he was drying off. That happened two more times. I gagged cleaning it all up.

You can't imagine what it is like getting him out of bed in the night or in the morning. I don't have to worry about his getting up without calling me anymore. He can't.

He will run out of antibiotic pills tomorrow and he is really not a lot better than he was three weeks ago, so I will call the doctor again. There is no comparison in the way he was walking when you were here over Memorial Day weekend and the way he is now. He usually does pretty good when he's been up and around, but when he's been lying down or sitting in a chair very long he can hardly walk. He blew the whistle for me and I went and helped him get into the bed. It was a struggle. This is hard for him. You can just imagine what it does to his morale.

I came up with an idea in the middle of the night that he approves of.

Our bathroom door opens back toward the toilet stool, and it is so hard for him to get around it. I suggested we take the door off and have it open the other way – or else I could make a "door" out of material in case we have company and people want privacy.

By changing the way the door swings or putting up a fabric curtain, Quentin could use his walker to get into the bathroom. As it is now, he has to use the cane to get into the bathroom, and that is not very satisfactory when he is so wobbly. At night I get a good grip on his pajamas to keep him up so he can use the urinal by the bed. In the daytime I keep him up by holding onto the back of his belt. We've got that worked out pretty good.

I also suggested putting a railing on the wall next to the stool, and he thought that was a good idea. We will get the materials when we go to town tomorrow. I'm also going to see about a "monkey bar" like they have on hospital beds to help a person get up. I want to see if I can get one that will work on his bed.

These gory details are not very interesting, but I just want you to know what it is like.

I have felt so good the last two days, and it is wonderful. Nothing has changed except my state of mind. I have been praying that we would have the faith to "Let Go and Let God." Don't know if I have told you the story about the man who fell over the edge of a cliff and was able to grab a small tree on the way down. He was in a very precarious position with a big ravine beneath him. He called out, "Lord, help me!"

The Lord answered, "Do you trust me?"

"Yes, Lord, I trust you."

"All right. Let go!"

After a few seconds the man called out, "Is there anyone else up there?"

I can really relate to that man. The other night as I struggled to get Quentin out of bed, it was all I could do to keep from crying. The thoughts were going through my mind as if they were on fast-forward. I was wondering how long can I keep doing this? What if I get down? Will he have to go to a wheelchair, or worse, a nursing home? I brought myself up short by thinking, "Let Go – Let God."

I still have the strength to get him up. He can still manage in the daytime. I just have to be thankful and have faith that the situation will take care of itself. I spent two or three days really concentrating on "Letting Go and Letting God," and it has helped. I pray every night that we will have increased faith, more wisdom and greater courage. It takes faith to use the guidance a person sometimes gets – like letting go.

I'm working diligently on exercises and my legs are doing better, so that is a help. The other night I had to use a heating pad to calm the jumpiness so I could sleep, and that was the first time in ages. I ride the bicycle and do a lot of stretches before going to bed. It takes me quite a while to get everything done. I really should start about 8:30, but I like to have some time in the evening to do what I want to do.

Delmar Knackstedt is going to work the ground for planting grass. I'm planning on making a huge flower garden of perennial flowers south of the house. I want them planted real close so the weeds can't grow in them. I have enjoyed the flowers so much this year, and it is imperative to have something pleasant and beautiful.

Hope everything is going well for you and that you and Annie thoroughly enjoy your new home. I think after a short time it will not seem so small to you. When it comes time to clean and redecorate, you will be grateful to not have so much square footage.

Lots of Love,

Mom

Tuesday, August 22, 1995

Dear Elaine,

I called the doctor's office this morning to let him know that Quentin was going to be out of antibiotic today, and I told them the diarrhea is no better. The nurse said the doctor was going to prescribe Elivel. I was amazed. I told her that he was already taking it. The doctor said to double the dose. I'm really not pleased about it.

This morning Quentin said that he feels like he's getting weaker every day. I can see it. He's asleep right now, so I'm going to go to town and get the material we need to make the safety rail next to toilet stool.

While I'm in town I'm going to go to the health food store and get some Bentonite. They told me the other day that it is good for diarrhea as it absorbs liquid. We have spent over $50 on prescription medicine, and it hasn't done one speck of good.

I'm in a hurry, so I'll write more later.

Love,

Mom

September 3, 1995

Dear Elaine,

Your dad is doing quite well. He's finally over the diarrhea. He has set a goal of two weeks to be rid of the walker. I don't discourage him or say anything negative; however, I'm afraid he'll be discouraged if he doesn't meet his goals. We are going to start water walking again at the Y next week. I still have to help him up at night, but it's not as hard as it was when he had diarrhea.

Greg came home and fixed the grab bar in the bathroom for Quentin. He also took the door off. It sure has made it easier. I regret that I didn't think of the grab bar sooner. It sure beats hanging on to the door knob with the door swinging back and forth. This helps him when he is dressing, too.

I'm looking forward to talking to you soon. I'm wondering about lots of things. How do Eric and Robert like Albuquerque? Have they both found jobs? Do you like their apartment? Is Annie getting excited about starting to school? Do you like your new boss? Did you get your house settled and organized to suit you? Have you been back to church?

Since Quentin is having such difficulty climbing stairs, we are thinking about trying the Christian or Methodist Church. The Christian Church has an elevator that goes to the second floor where the classrooms are as well as to the basement to their Fellowship Hall.

I think the United Church of Christ (Congregational) and the Christian Church are going to be uniting. I'm wondering how they will work out the business of baptism. The Christian Church dunks the people who want to be Christians. That is completely alien, and I think probably unacceptable to Congregationalists. It certainly would be to Quentin.

I've been dunked by the Christians, sprinkled by the Catholics, and I have signed the register at the Congregational Church. I should be "saved" don't you think?

At the Christian Church they have communion every Sunday. The Congregationalists thought they were being put upon when Judith started having communion once a month instead of once every three months. We might have to visit the Presbyterian Church. It's all on one floor. I've heard the Methodists come visit you at home and try to make the decision for you as to how much you give to the church. We wouldn't like that either.

I've been reading an interesting book entitled, *God Will Work With You but Not For You*. It is written by a woman named Lao Russell. She feels our world is on the brink of collapse and that it is up to women to save it. She said God made everything in pairs – male and female. They each have a job but are supposed to be equal. She feels very strongly that women need to be in government and in executive positions. This book was written in 1955, before the women's liberation movement.

It's interesting to hear what is going on in China now with the women's gathering. One of the best programs I ever attended was presented by a participant in the last U.N. Women's Conference. She told how they brought a group of Arab women and a group of Israeli women together in a forum. At first there was a lot of antagonism, but as they talked they came to the conclusion that they both wanted peace. They wanted to be able to send their children off to school and feel confident that they would come home at night. They wanted to feel secure in their homes, and they wanted their husbands to be safe. By the time it was over the antagonism was gone.

She also told about women who lived in the South Pacific area talking about all the nuclear testing going on there and what it was doing to their lives. The women came to the conclusion that just because men went to war, it was very much a woman's business, as they had to suffer the loss of husbands and sons and had to keep things going while they were away.

I would sure like to be able to hear a report on this U.N. Meeting of Women in China. I hope to be able to get a lot of it on cable. I would love to be involved somehow, but at this stage of the game I can only watch and read and pray.

I wish you could see my Vincas. They are beautiful! I have never liked Vincas very much – they seemed so precise. I learned there are two kinds – and I bought the good kind. One thing I really like about them is that you don't ever have to remove dead blossoms. When they have done their job, they just drop off. Instead of having one blossom, these have three at one place. When one disappears I think two more come out. I'm going to have more of them next year.

This morning I looked out and saw a Blue Jay taking his bath, and before long there was a beautiful big red bird. He took a long time deciding if he wanted to get in that water or not, but he finally took a nice leisurely bath. When I looked out and saw him, I almost gasped. We will probably get a lot of interesting birds during the migration season. I'm putting out fresh water for them morning and night. It makes the kitchen work more interesting.

Well, it is almost midnight and it will soon be time for Quentin to wake up and use the urinal. He had tried to get by without calling me, but it was such an ordeal for him that he would be wet before he could get up. Last night he called me five times! He did stay dry, though. I started him back on Saw Palmetto today, which is a product from the health food store. It's used very widely by men with prostate trouble. Going to the bathroom so frequently is one of the side effects of prostate cancer. He sure is working hard to get well. He is working his hand and arm and says it feels stronger.

Tuesday, September 6, 1995

I did not get this finished last night, so will try now. We went in to water walk at the Y this morning and enjoyed it. Quentin wants to go walk in the park this evening and continue to do his therapy at home. We go to Salina tomorrow. We have a 9:00 am appointment with the urologist. That is terribly early for us, but we will make it. Since it is our 53rd anniversary, we might try to work in something special.

I thought and prayed about your kids a lot yesterday. I'm sure glad Robert has such a strong work ethic and is getting a good start with Target. Eric ought to be able to get a job without any trouble.

You mentioned that we all have our own destiny. I don't believe we are destined to have certain things happen to us. I firmly believe that we make choices and decisions that affect our lives. I think we are allowed to make choices that are not right, and then we are allowed to learn from them. We can either make corrections, let things get worse – or stay the same (which is sometimes bad enough).

Christy is having a Home Interior Party tonight, but I'm not going. I think I could leave Quinten safely now, but would be uncomfortable, as I know he would feel awfully lonesome. I would enjoy being with other people and would like to see Christy's new house, but I hate those parties. A person always feels obligated to buy, and I get so mad at myself when I do that. I never use what I have bought – might be because I buy the cheapest thing in the catalog.

I have a pair of wooden candle sconces that are still in the box—ditto for the magazine rack—ditto for some metal butterflies. Have used some of the scented candles I bought once, but that was years ago and still have over half of them.

Quentin has just come to the living room to say, 'Let's eat." Better go. Hope everything is going well for you.

Lots of love,

Mom

September 17, 1995

Dear Elaine,

I feel I have some good news. It seems to me that Quentin is improving. He walked out in our gravel driveway today and did real well. It has not been too long ago that I had to hold on to the back of his belt when he walked to give him security. He rode the bicycle this morning. We will go into the Y tomorrow. I think that has helped him a lot. I'm so grateful to the company that gave the $3,000 for the purchase of an electric lift chair. He would not be able to get into or out of the swimming pool if it weren't for that.

He has been terribly emotional lately. He has just cried and cried since we got the letter from Jennifer. All a person has to do is say, "We got a letter from Jennifer," and he starts crying. He was crying when we talked to you the other evening. He held the telephone away from his mouth when he was crying so you wouldn't hear him. He hates it when he cries. He said that Jennifer's letters bring back so many memories of the service and the war.

I told you that Delmar came and worked the ground so we could plant grass. I spent most of my afternoon watering. Got an oscillating sprinkler that has adjustments on it, which is really nice. This water is so terrible that I don't want it hitting the house and turning the paint rust-colored. Sure glad I didn't start this job when the temperatures were over 100 every day.

Have I told you Christy gave Quentin a crew cut? He looks like a cross between a new recruit and a skinhead— a little more like a skinhead. He likes it, and I really think he looks good. She cuts Rock's hair all the time. I'm grateful she's willing to do Quentin's, too. It will save $9.50 and the nuisance of going to the barber shop and getting in and out of the barber chair.

I was thinking about my birthday this evening and

remembered that just two years ago I was at a Healing Seminar at Unity. I had such a wonderful time. Quentin and Gene played twenty-seven holes of golf that day.

Speaking of Unity, we are reading the book, *Lessons in Truth*, which is a basic Unity textbook. It was first published in 1894, and is still used in the ministry and teaching programs. The truths written in there unchanging. Quentin listens while I read a chapter every night. He wants me to read to him, but he gets awfully fidgety before I get through. He doesn't understand it very well, but it is a start. I had not read the book through completely for a long time and am enjoying it very much.

I will be interested in talking to you about your trip and other things.

Lots of love,

Mom

October 1, 1995

Dear Elaine,

It is almost 10:30, and I am wilting fast, so don't know how long I will write tonight. Your dad is already in bed. We went to town and walked in the park across from the fire department tonight. He did the best job of walking he has done since having the stroke. He walked east almost a block and then had to turn around and go back west. He didn't drag his foot a single time. He was absolutely exhausted when he got to the car but elated.

We came home and he tried to resume reading a book he has been working on diligently for over three weeks. He was so tired he couldn't concentrate. At 9:00 he said he had read the last chapter three times and still didn't know what it said, so he went to bed.

I am working hard keeping the ground watered so the grass seed will grow. I picked up a couple seeds tonight and they both had little roots on them, so it shouldn't be much longer before I will be seeing green grass.

I don't think I have told you that hereinafter, the area south of the house will be called the "courtyard." If everything works out right, it will really be a pretty and enjoyable place next summer. I have been told perennials don't bloom very well the first year. I have also been told if I want flowers that bloom the whole season that I need to plant some annuals. I will have both.

Your dad feels so bad that he can't help. Of course, he wouldn't want to help in the garden even if he were able to. It's an absolute disaster. I had kept it up all summer until he got in such bad shape from the diarrhea. I could not be pulling him out of bed three times a night, cleaning up messes, and hoeing the garden during the day. He was my first priority. When we were driving out of the yard yesterday I was talking about the garden. He said, "Wait a little while until I am strong enough, and I will take care of it."

I do feel so bad for him. He forgets that he can't do things, and he is always saying, "I'll do that for you," and then he feels terrible when he can't.

Lots of love,

Mom

October 3, 1995

Dear Elaine,

I was so thrilled when I went out this morning and could see a lot of green just barely peeping through. The forecast was for it to be terribly windy, so I watered the whole lawn real well. When we came home from Salina this afternoon there were dry patches, but the grass had grown. Quentin looked out the window and said the lawn had almost a green cast.

Quentin had to go the urologist in Salina today. We went to Earthcare in the afternoon and I got some more bulbs. I got some anemones, crocus and some more daffodils and tulips. I'm going to start a lot of plants from seed. I'm sure having fun. I told Quentin that I could see one reason I have never done this – it does get expensive.

I have had an interesting situation. One day several weeks ago I went to town to go to a Meals on Wheels board meeting. There were only three of us there so the meeting was called off. I had some books to take to the library, and at the stop sign I saw my friend Norma

Tucker in a car with Mary Glidden. They called out to me asking about Eleanor Clark. There wasn't any traffic, so I went out and talked to them.

I told Norma I had almost called her to have coffee when the Meals on Wheels meeting was called off, but I remembered that she had coffee with a group of women on Friday morning. She and Mary invited me to join them, and I did. This is a very prestigious group of women, and they are so much fun. I was invited to Mary Lynn Bowker's when she had the group at her home, and then about three weeks ago Lucy Johnson called me up to say she was having the group at her home and wanted me to come – so I did.

I feel like I am crashing the party all the time, but they have certainly made me feel welcome. Now I look forward to coffee every Friday morning.

I'm glad you like your work. I love hearing the stories about all of the people at the station. It must be interesting working with people from so many different countries and backgrounds.

Lots of love,

Mom

October 14, 1995

Dear Elaine,

On Friday I was to go to a board meeting for Meals on Wheels. I was also invited to Lucille Miller's house for Coffee. I wouldn't have missed that gathering for anything. Lucille's home is beautiful. She has a woman who travels with them from one home to the other. (They have three houses that are all just exactly alike.) She had a beautiful brunch and her "woman" served the coffee and passed the various kinds of food for second helpings. It was very pleasant.

I was amused at Jayne and Lucille. Jayne commented on my black patent shoes with the gold trim. Something was said about them being expensive. Lucille said, "Sometimes when I feel like I can't afford to buy two pairs because they are expensive, I wait and go back the next day and buy the second pair."

Jayne said she did the same thing, or sometimes she would use two different credit cards.

Quentin has given up driving voluntarily. He does drive up to Larry's shop, and he drove over to Conway the other day. I'm so happy that it has not been one of those heart-wrenching situations. He had mentioned one time that he could drive us to Albuquerque to see you, and I said I wouldn't go with him. He wanted to know why, and I said that his coordination was not good enough – and it isn't.

It's even hard for him to use the remote control for the TV. He pushes the red "off" button when he wants to change stations. He will swear something is wrong with the control when all he has to do is push the volume either up or down. We would never make it to Albuquerque.

I had trouble sleeping on Thursday night thinking about the fact that I have never been afraid of dying. I finally came to the conclusion that it might have been because of my whooping cough when I was three months old. The priest was called to give me last rites. I have always had a spiritual nature and, as you know, have often said that the physical world is not all that wonderful in my opinion. I wonder if I had some kind of "crossing over" experience that I just don't remember.

We're so glad your work and everything is going well for you. I can appreciate how grateful your employees are to you for teaching them the television business. It must be fun for all of you to be setting new sales records. I've thought all week about the way some of the male clients have treated your young saleswomen. It's disgusting that they think these women are "hot to trot" just because they are Hispanic.

I also did a lot of thinking last week about the comments Annie made about men not being attracted to you. I think Annie came to a lot of the right conclusions, but I have some additional thoughts. I think you are used to dealing with successful, well-to-do men all the time, and you are not overwhelmed when you meet one socially. They probably don't get the homage and adulation they are used to and want.

Jennifer has said that under certain circumstances she would "act blonde." That is probably what most of them want. However, I'm sure you want a person who can be comfortable and accepting of a woman who is intelligent and successful. As you well know, there are worse things than being single – and one is being married to the wrong person.

I can remember reading an interview with Barbara Walters. She said she was on a plane going home one night when it struck her that there wasn't anyone who cared whether she got home or not. I think she started putting out feelers, and it wasn't too long before she was married. Her husband was very opinionated, and she tried to please him. He didn't like the way she dressed. For a while she was dressing very inappropriately (in my opinion) for her age. Her hair style was changed frequently and looked like a style too young for her (in my opinion). Since she got her divorce she has dressed appropriately and worn her hair appropriately and looks better in every way (in my opinion).

I have always said I wouldn't marry again, but I'm even more adamant about it now. I would never love anyone else enough to go through the last two years. I had the thought recently that I have all the disadvantages of not having a husband and all the disadvantages of having one. Marg was over one day and was bemoaning the fact that she has to make all the decisions and take care of everything on her own. So do I.

I am also very tied down and am restricted in what I can do. I could write a whole page of all the things I have to do that a single woman would not have to do. Last Friday night I had to get up at 2:00 am and strip Quentin's bed down to and including the rubber sheet and start over. At 6:00 am he was wet again, and I had to do it all over again.

The other day we went to town and bought a new doorknob for the dining room. He started on it right after lunch. Finally he got so frustrated I told him to go take a nap. He worked on it again after supper. He got up on Saturday morning and started on it again. Every few minutes he was calling me to get something for him. Teri stopped by after lunch, and we were both so glad to see her. She finished it up in just a little bit. That's the type of thing he used to be able to fix without even thinking.

He is getting stronger and most days he's been able to get up in time to relieve himself. The other morning he called me, and I rushed to the bedroom just as he was slipping to the floor. He sat there a while, and eventually I was able to get him up on his knees. We used the hoist to bring him into a standing position. I was surprised that he didn't have an *accident*, but he was able to get up and use the urinal. I think the swimming is making him a lot stronger.

Lots of love,

Mom

November 5, 1995

Dear Annie:

HAPPY 16th BIRTHDAY! I'm sorry I'm late. Your mother and I rather expect that of each other, but you probably aren't old enough to appreciate the fine art of procrastination yet. I do hope you have had a good day.

I liked this card because of the little dancer. I still remember going to your dance program in Colorado Springs and how much I enjoyed it. You were so graceful. It was beautiful. Then there was that little boy who had a lot of enthusiasm but not a lot of skill. I laughed and laughed about him. I'm so glad I got to go to that. It is the only thing I ever got to do with you.

I went to the wrestling tournaments and different kinds of ball games with your brothers. I've gone to programs at the country school for Christy and Candi and their high school graduations. I went to some kind of a carnival at Jennifer and Danny's school and a Christmas program when they lived here. I enjoyed your dance program most of all, and I'm so glad it worked out that I was there at the right time.

Your mother said you were going for another job interview today. I hope you get it. I was in the mall in Hutchinson not too long ago. It has really suffered since Wal-Mart moved out. The Cookie Factory was closed. I wonder if your old boss got to the place where he couldn't find girls he could domineer and under-pay.

I hope you like your new school. Your mother said today that she had been very impressed with the principal and your teachers. I think she would have liked an alternative high school. I remember her saying once something about the teachers not treating the students like they were people – or intelligent – or something to that effect.

I didn't have any trouble being a teenager. As a matter of fact, I enjoyed it. At my fortieth class reunion we were supposed to relate something funny that had happened in high school. Some of the "kids" told stories that made us laugh so hard we had tears running down our faces.

When it was my turn I said I couldn't remember anything funny, but I went on to say that my high school years had been the happiest time of my life. I admitted I wouldn't have said that if Quentin had been with me (he was harvesting wheat.) A little bit later one of the girls said, "Tell Quentin to not feel bad. My husband says the best time of his life was during the War."

I also made the comment I felt we were lucky to have been teenagers before World War II, as the world has been so different since then. Everyone there nodded his/her head in agreement. Our world was certainly nothing like the one you are confronted with now. I would like to go back to having the kind of social standards we had then. Although I would hate to have to give up TV, microwaves, automatic washers and driers, air conditioning, electric mixers, electric knives, dishwashers and computers. (We didn't even have electric typewriters.)

Probably ninety-eight percent of the kids didn't smoke, drink or indulge in sex, but we had lots of fun. I can't ever remember saying, "I'm bored." I used to get so mad at Christy and Candi when they said that. I could (and usually did) give them a long list of things they could be doing so they wouldn't be bored. As I recall, they didn't appreciate or follow my suggestions.

Going back to your school. I would certainly stress computer courses (if you haven't already had them). I have said in the past that I think all girls should be required to have typing and bookkeeping. I used to say shorthand, but I don't think that is used nearly as much now. All of those subjects are basic and would be helpful even if you married a very rich man and never worked.

I don't know how I would have gotten by without a typewriter all these years. I have done the bookkeeping for the farm for forty-nine years now. I have also been treasurer and secretary of a number of organizations. I once knew a woman who graduated from college with a degree in business administration and could not type!

We're looking forward to Thanksgiving and getting to see you and your mother. We're sorry the boys won't be able to get off work that long. I know you and the boys are glad to be back in the same town again. I would also guess that you enjoy having Robert stay at the house when you mother has to be gone on her business trips.

We love you and wish the very best for you—not only for the next year but for always.

Lots of Love,

Grandma

Chapter 3 - 1996

January 4, 1996

Dear Elaine,

I'm glad you enjoyed our little book *Seems Like Yesterday*. Quentin and I had a lot of fun writing it. It's funny how our memories of dating and World War II are still so vivid after all these years. The other kids acted like they were delighted when we gave them out, but no one has made any comments since then. Maybe they didn't think it was much of a Christmas present, or maybe they haven't read it yet.

I think I might write about different isolated events and possibly just for you. There are some very difficult years of just plain hard grubbing work and poverty that I don't care to remember any more than I can help.

There is nothing very inspirational about remembering when it was a major catastrophe when Larry would need a quarter for lunch for a field trip – or when I had to learn to not cross my legs when I went to Child Study Club because I had holes in the bottom of my shoes – or when I had to crawl straight up that ladder on the vestibule wall in the milk barn to push the grain over the holes for the cows and then have rats come down those feeders with the grain. I didn't like being hit in the face with the cows' tails that had great big knots of mud and shit – or washing the crud off teats – or scraping the shit out of the barn. Really there was nothing about any of it that I liked.

Well, that part is over, and I don't think I am any the worse for it. Thank God it was during that time that I found Unity. That made so much difference in my life. Don't think I could ever have survived the following years if it hadn't been for the many lessons I learned from them. It is still helping me survive.

I enjoyed the paper you sent with the story about Alex and also the annual report from his college. He's very handsome. I wouldn't have guessed he was Mexican. His ideas on the school sound very solid and worthwhile. I'm sure I would find him fascinating and interesting. I would probably feel very intimidated around him since he's a college president. Guess I would have to take the attitude that Wimpy, the cartoon character had. He said, "I yam what I yam and that is all that I yam."

I thought about Alex last Sunday morning when we were watching Meet the Press. Their chief photographer is ninety-seven years old. He's been with Meet the Press for forty-eight years. He started taking pictures when Woodrow Wilson was president. I think people who use their mental abilities and have an interesting life live longer than ones who beat themselves to death with physical work. Of course, a person's genes make a difference.

Speaking of marriage – which we weren't. At this stage of my life, I cannot see why a woman (you in particular) would want to give up freedom for marriage. When I was your age I would have probably felt a lot different. I think men are basically selfish and expect a woman to give up herself for them. Men who have been alone and have taken care of themselves very well suddenly become extremely helpless when they get married. They can also become very demanding about a person's time.

I guess I'm feeling sorry for myself as I am so terribly tied down. Thank God your dad still has a great disposition and his mind is good – not as sharp as he used to be – but considering he is not involved in anything that demands his attention or concentration, I think he is doing well.

You seem to be using good judgment in this matter with not rushing into it. I do worry about the age difference, though. You've seen what I've gone through, so if this relationship goes further and you decide to marry Alex, do it with your eyes open. You could be a young woman taking care of an old, sick man for a very long time.

I think when a person has a sick wife or husband it can feel as if you've been alone for the same number of years that person was sick. I have said that my husband died on October 30, 1993. We just haven't gotten around to burying him yet. Hopefully Quentin will die first. It will probably take some time for me to remember what it was like before his stroke. Then the grief will start.

Well, Quentin has shut off the TV so that means he is ready to go to bed.

Love,

Mom

Tuesday, January 9, 1996

Dear Elaine,

Quentin urgently wanted me to tell both you and Alex that you are at an age when "something" could happen any time. I asked if that was a warning in general – a warning about getting married or a warning that you had better be enjoying life to the fullest. He said it was the latter. You are really quite young – a wonderful age – and Quentin did not seem old when he was 61.

I cannot help but wonder if Quentin's stroke could have been avoided if he hadn't worked so hard that last summer. He would get so desperately tired. I could not get him to say "enough" as he felt that Larry needed him so much. He also went around for years with high blood pressure. He insisted that high blood pressure was normal for him. Marg told him once it might be normal for him, but it wasn't normal. I finally got him to go to the doctor for a physical. As we were turning into the clinic he said, "I expect him to find that I have high blood pressure."

I asked him why he felt that way. He explained that he had a pounding in his temples. He did have high blood pressure and was put on medication immediately. I nearly exploded. I reminded him that he had always been afraid of a stroke and then he was guilty of harboring a condition that could cause one. He was very good about taking his medication and always took responsibility for it. I never had to remind him to take it. I think he had been taking it for at least two years before he had the stroke.

It has sure played hell with our lives – especially his. Sometimes I can get to feeling sorry for poor Madelyn about being tied down, but it doesn't take long to think how much worse it is for him. He has the choice of sleeping, reading or watching TV. He was terribly depressed last night. For two days he was incontinent day and night.

Last night he said the only thing that kept him from committing suicide was the fact that I was so opposed to it. He was brought up to believe suicide was an honorable thing to do under some circumstances. From everything I have read concerning communication from people on the "other side", they do not escape any misery and might just as well have faced the situation here. In addition to that, I can't think of a meaner thing a person can do to the family. That is the thing I have stressed to Quentin, and he says that's the only thing that keeps him from doing it.

We talk about death quite often. When he brings the subject up I go ahead and pursue it. It was my belief when I was a very young woman that if a person really loved someone, she would release him if he were in an incurable or painful condition. I still feel that way. I also know that life goes on, and I cannot understand why people think they can't.

I have always felt that the three years Quentin was overseas during the War taught me a lot about being separated from a loved one. I don't think I will be guilty of expressing the standard wifely things that seem to be expected. They make me want to gag. Such as, "Well, at least I could sit and watch him"…(suffer?) "We always did everything together. I just don't know what I'll do." (Good grief!) We all know that one of us will be going – usually the husband – and we had damned well better be able to do a few things alone.

I would guess the fact that I am so independent could be making it harder for me now. I continue to try to use this time as a growing experience and a time to really express love. I'm sure I've told you that I have prayed I would be willing to be a channel for God's love and caring. I feel I have been. Often I feel like I'm not the one taking the action. I guess I do the action, but I'm not the instigator. It is an interesting experience.

I was so pleased to hear about the kids the other night.

It is amazing the way people choose their careers. I would never have expected Eric to be in the restaurant business, but it can be a very rewarding, interesting career. I would not have expected Robert to be happy with Target, but he probably has a good future there, or at least is doing important ground work for a position in the future.

I did not know that Annie had the artistic talent, but I'm excited about her getting the training for the animation work. I can visualize all kinds of interesting things in her future. If a person's ability is channeled, there are many opportunities. You had mentioned that Annie did so well in Colorado Springs when she was a co-emcee for a school program. I remember her poise and ability when she was in that dance program, so I can well imagine how she did a great job of modeling too. Hope she doesn't get side-tracked with someone (male) at an early age. Can you believe an old woman like me not thinking that getting married and having children early is the best thing that could happen to a woman?

Well, I hear Quentin sneezing again and he might be about ready to go to bed, so I'll sign off. So glad that everything is going well for you. I love to hear about the many activities with your work and with Alex and the kids. I think it is so interesting that you felt so drawn to Albuquerque, even before you got this job.

Lots and Lots of Love,

Mom

February 19, 1996

Dear Elaine,

We are looking forward to having you come – any time. If you come in March there will be a lot less work and possibly strain. You will be most welcome whenever you can come – with or without Alex. We are both anticipating meeting him.

I'm feeling encouraged about your dad. It seems to me that he is coming back to life. His eyes and face in general are more like they used to be. He even wakes up laughing and joking in the morning at times and I am always so thrilled. I would be happy to have him regain some other abilities, but maybe that will come eventually.

Next week is national "Random Acts of Kindness Week." I haven't seen anything about it except in my *Unity* magazine. Unity is stressing it. I have had fun thinking of various people I would like to drop a note of appreciation to.

I'm trying to dig out some closets, drawers and places that have been neglected for many years. I'm slow at it, but every little bit helps and encourages me to do more. I have a mess around the computer and promise myself every day that I will get to it, but haven't so far. Making decisions about keeping or destroying papers is a big deal to me. Guess I love the printed word so much that it is hard to part with anything.

I've decided I had better really get busy on developing some good habits that will come in handy now and later on. They really are pretty basic things – like closing a cupboard door when I have gotten what I want. As you know, I can finish preparing toast and juice for breakfast and have the kitchen looking like a tornado has struck.

I read an article in the Unity magazine recently that I thought was so good. If I recall correctly, a young monk had just gone to the monastery. He asked an older one what he could do. He was asked if he had eaten. He replied yes. The older monk said, "Wash your dish."

There were some similar stories – the point being to do what is there to be done. That has been especially meaningful to me. I'm trying to train myself to make a list of what I need in town so one trip will do the job instead of two or three. It is obvious I won't run out of anything to do or learn for the rest of my life!

Look forward so much to seeing you – anytime. Wish I could add any place, but it will have to be here for now.

Lots of love,

Mom

April 4, 1996

Dear Elaine,

I had a pleasant surprise this morning. I looked out the dining room window, as I always do, and saw a yellow blossom. I dressed very hurriedly, got a heavy coat on and went out to inspect it. It was not completely opened, but it was a daffodil. A lot of the other daffodils had buds on them. They aren't very tall. Only about four crocus plants came up, and the rabbits ate them off as soon as they popped out. It has been so cold. I'm hoping the tulips will emerge before long.

We enjoyed getting your letter and the pictures. The house looks very interesting. I know what you mean about the "mud hut" architecture now. Your Sandia Mountains don't quite compare to Pike's Peak, but they probably change colors with the various times of day and the weather. I'm sure you enjoy looking at them. I'm so glad Annie enjoyed the prom. She sure takes a good photograph. She's very glamorous and exotic looking.

Quentin and I have been walking in town every day that is even barely warm enough. It was rather cold and terribly windy yesterday, but we are fairly well protected in the park.

We are looking forward to hearing your schedule and anticipating having you and Alex here.

Lots and lots of love,

Mom

April 9, 1996

Dear Elaine,

I have to write this letter quickly (as if I ever have). I have Quentin tucked in bed. We go to town in the morning for a fasting blood profile, then we are going to Salina. He has his cancer shot at 2:00. I want to stop by Earth Care and Sam's before he gets his shot.

I think the damned animals must have killed my tulips, as they have not even come up. I have enjoyed the jonquils, but they are ready to be cut down. The hyacinths are beautiful, but there are only four. The rest were eaten off by varmints. I'm going to buy some things at Earth Care since I have quite a lot of money left from the gift you gave me last fall.

The flowering pear tree you gave me started blossoming yesterday. It is leafed out so nice. It doesn't have enough blossoms yet to be breath-taking, but it is getting there. I bought a barberry bush and one rugosa rose bush last week. Greg planted them for me yesterday. He also took the bottle of Round-Up and sprayed some areas where I wanted the weeds killed. I wish I could have him for several days to do some special things for me.

I especially enjoyed having Jean and Frank here. I had gotten into a rather unpleasant emotional state, but I feel like I am back on an even keel now. When you were here you said I needed to take a day a week off. I was busy getting some extra things done and just didn't get around to taking any time for myself. I had reached a stage where everything about Quentin irritated me.

I hated the way he huffed and puffed when he got in bed. It irritated me to distraction over the way that he would never get up far enough on the bed to lay down in the right place. He would also lay down completely cross-ways in the bed with his feet still off the bed. The huffing and puffing to get turned to the right place was enough to "blow the house down."

It didn't start my morning off right to get up and find a very wet Depend and a pair of wet shorts and pajamas on the floor and urine dripping off the rubber bed pad onto the floor. I wanted to scream when he would sit and watch me put the orange juice, medication and vitamins, etc. on the table. When I would come with the toast, he acted surprised that it was time for breakfast, and then he had to go through a struggle to get his chair located right. I wanted to scream, "Why in the hell do you put so many pills in your hand when you drop some of them each morning?"

I don't have time to remember and itemize all the other irritants. I do realize that the stroke has affected him in so many ways that aren't obvious. I also know he is definitely not this way by choice and that he is not trying to irritate me. That is the reason I don't want to be cross with him. I also realize that some day I might be in even worse condition. I feel it is important "to do unto others as you would have them do unto you." It would be awful to be struggling with every little thing and have your caretaker and others cross with you.

There is a celebration this Saturday in Hutchinson of the fiftieth anniversary of the Kansas Holstein Association. There will be a show in the morning and then a lunch at noon. All the "old timers" have been given a special invitation to come. Delmar Conner called and wanted to know if we could possibly attend.

When Delmar was telling me about all the "old timers" who were supposed to be there, I had an interesting experience. It seemed that all the different shows and sales were grouped into one big memory, and I felt so aware of all the people who used to attend. The impression was of a beautiful day in a place with bleacher seats, an atmosphere of fun and friendliness. I got off the phone and let Quentin talk to Delmar.

When he hung up I was crying, I told Quentin I wanted to go. He cried too. My poor sister and Frank were sitting there wondering what had happened. Jean looked so sympathetic and asked what had happened. Sounded kind of silly to say I was just painfully reminded of a different time and different circumstances.

A couple nights later Quentin asked me why I had

cried, and I told him. He said he would go, but he has been worrying about it ever since. He is so concerned that he will wet his pants. Candi said to take a small throw and put it on the back of the wheelchair. If he has an accident, put it over his lap as if he were cold. That might not play so well if the temperature is 90 or so. One time he told me he would go and stay until he wet his pants, and then we would leave. I'm going to go even if he doesn't.

I wrote to Ed Reed and told him there was a piece of history I thought should be tucked away in the Association history. Quentin came home from the service in October of 1945. Dale and Grandpa Stan had kept Quentin's herd together during the war. Quentin went to the State Fair in the fall of 1946. He had the Grand Champion cow and took first in the Three Females Bred and Owned by an Exhibitor, plus a lot of other firsts. Larry was about three weeks old, so I didn't go to the fair. It was fairly late that evening when he came home, but he was jubilant.

There was a Professor Atkinson from Kansas State University who was very active and wanted to promote the Holsteins of Kansas. He was the instigator of getting a group of the Kansas breeders to go to Waterloo, Iowa, which was the ultimate goal at that time. Quentin went and was so thrilled when he placed third in the Three Females Bred and Owned by the Exhibitor. Maytag Farms was first, Pabst was second, and Quentin Kubin from Kansas was third. People were going around saying, "Who the hell is Quentin Kubin?" He was really hooked from that time on.

I have been thinking of the many things that could be said about Quentin. He was recognized in the *National Holstein World Magazine* as a "masterful showman." Delmar Conner got his basic start from cattle purchased from us, as well as Gib Kaufman, who is still in the business and recognized for fabulous production. A number of people purchased bulls from us that turned out real well. If they give him the credit and recognition he deserves, he will probably cry. It will be interesting to see what happens.

April 10,

You will be relieved to know that I am patient and loving with Quentin again. I have been, and will continue to be, aggressive about insisting that he walks with his heel down. He is not walking nearly as well as he did before the knee surgery. It occurred to me today that his knee surgery has nothing to do with the way he is walking. His knees are fine. Tonight I told Quentin I felt he could do much better.

He admitted when Dr. Harbin told him that stroke victims sometimes have to use a walker for the rest of their lives that it had taken the wind out of his sails. I told him he ought to prove to the doctor that he was not one of those victims.

Teri and Candi were talking about Quentin yesterday morning. Candi told me when Larry asks him to go check a field that he drives to the field, gets out of the pickup, walks through the ditch and out to the field – without a walker! They both feel he has the ability, but they think he's in a state of depression that keeps him from having the push he needs to make the exertion for aggressive exercising.

Teri said the boys were all wimps and that none of them will face their Dad's condition. She and Candi said you are the only one of the "kids" who will tell it like it is. They feel there was a big difference in him after you were home at Thanksgiving time and talked about putting him in a nursing home.

I had an inspiration since I started writing this that will need consideration and probably careful handling. I want you to think about it. Quentin will not work hard at getting well for himself, but I'm thinking he might do it for me if he thought it was important for my well-being. It might be a little hard to make him see that I need help, considering the gardening and other things I am doing, but is something to keep on the back burner and think about.

I have lost almost ten pounds since Christmas. Dr. Quamar told me once that I would probably get my triglicerides down if I lost weight. My reading was 381 and 100 is the acceptable – or desirable reading.

Also, I decided to lose weight so I could justify buying a few new clothes. I have bought very few in the last six years. The ones I had were good. When a person's life is restricted to the grocery store and church, the clothes are certainly not abused and they don't show wear. Lots of my clothes are now ten years old.

This would probably sound ridiculous to most people, but I feel free to tell you. I feel that I have had some spiritual help in this effort. It has been so easy, and I'm eating very well – just not over-eating. Things like ice cream, candy and cookies just don't appeal to me any more. I very often eat a half a grapefruit while Quentin is eating ice cream. I feel better and it doesn't feel like I'm sacrificing anything. I'm grateful for the help. I will give the Spirit credit, rather than saying I finally have some sense at seventy-two after years and years of struggling with weight.

If I'm going to get any sleep tonight I'd better stop writing and go to bed. I'll be in touch.

Love,

Mom

May 13, 1996

Dear Elaine,

I went to Morris and Son this afternoon to check on a white pleated skirt I had seen in the window. I didn't buy the skirt. However, I saw this little angel pin and could not resist buying it for you. Take it to Spain with you. I went to the library today and checked out the book you told me about. I looked up Washington Irving and was pleased to see they had *Tales of the Alhambra*. I am looking forward to reading it.

I'm sure pleased with the progress your dad has made. He has not had to use the hoist for at least two weeks, and he can get in bed without huffing and puffing. Since he has control of his bladder, it makes it easier for both of us. He said the other day he felt like life was worth living again. He doesn't use the walker most of the time. He is working real hard to keep his heel down on his right foot. I have to give him some rather stern encouragement like, "Get that damned heel down!" It seems to be working.

I read that we have little root-like things called dendrites in our brain. The article stated that people can grow new dendrites to replace some that are lost from a stroke – or even old age. The secret is to develop some new habits. It seems that one good way is to exercise, develop a new hobby or to get very interested in something different – something a person enjoys. My flowers are my new hobby. As I was working with the hoses this morning and trying to screw them together again, I couldn't help but wonder if learning how to screw in hoses would help grow dendrites.

I hope you like your little angel as much as I do. I think she is such a beautiful little thing. Wear her when you are flying – at least. For a country girl, you sure do get around – Germany, England, Spain. I would have loved it at your age, but at this stage of life, I would be very happy to travel in the United States.

We really like Alex. He seemed to enjoy the trip to Kansas, so I don't think you'll have to worry about him getting moody or acting like a jerk in Spain. He's certainly a lot different from the other men you've had in your life.

Have a good time and God Bless,

Lots of love,

Mom

June 1, 1996

Dear Elaine,

Thought I would write and bring you up to date. Nothing exciting or traumatic has happened. Your dad is about the same – some days better than others. We continue to go to town to walk, and he is doing the leg exercises. I use a very good vibrator at night and massage his legs. Last night we went to town and walked two blocks – one down one back. He was exhausted and had to struggle to get into the car. Today his legs have been weak. He says he walked too much yesterday.

We've had quite a bit of rain and humidity and he is having a terrible time breathing. We go to the doctor on Thursday, and I'm going to see if we should change his medication. He has been taking this particular pill for breathing for over two years. I'm ready to start trying some herbs. I will probably have to make him think it's a prescription or he'll be sure it couldn't possibly help. The prescription he takes for his breathing is $70.00 for 100 pills. If it were helping it would be fine.

I now weigh 143 most of the times. Sometimes I get to 142, which is my goal. It is interesting how I meet people who immediately exclaim that I have lost a lot of weight. There has not been a peep out of Teri, the girls or any of the family. I just ignore the fact that they ignore me. I think I look good.

You asked if I were anorexic. I'm not. I do exercises every night and get to the swimming pool at least two times a week, and I really give myself a good workout there. I feel like I look real good now, as long as I keep my top covered up. My ribs and the clavicle bones are very visible. Losing 27 pounds has not improved the appearance of my bust. Sometimes I think I look like a bitch dog that's just finished nursing a litter of 10 pups. My upper arms are quite wrinkled. Otherwise, I look great.

A friend asked me last week how I had accomplished the weight loss. I told her I had cut out fatty foods and sweets. I also told her it helps to have a semi-invalid husband.

Greg will be here next week to fly on some milo seed for Larry. It has rained so much he hasn't been able to plant. We are looking forward to seeing Greg and his new $450,000 airplane. That will be fun! It is going to be fun to talk to you – probably tomorrow. I checked out a book on Spain and Quentin and I looked at it tonight.

Sunday

It was fun talking to you on the phone this morning. I'm pleased about your engagement, and as you know, we are wishing you many years of happiness.

As I was preparing the duckling for dinner this morning, I was thinking I was having such a good dinner we should share it. I asked the minister if he would like to come out – and he did. I could tell that he was older than his wife. I asked today how many children they had. He said they had each been married before. He had five by his first wife and she had two. I guess I bluntly asked if he was quite a bit older than her. Turns out he is 18 years older and they have been married 20 years.

By doing some advanced math, I figured out that he was 53 when they got married. I also asked him if it had worked out well. He said that so far it had been great. He said they both realized he would probably die before she did, but they have enjoyed the years they have been together.

Have to stop writing so I can beat the mailman to the mailbox.

Love,

Mom

June 21, 1996

Dear Elaine,

I have been watering the "courtyard" most of the day. I finally learned how to adjust the spray arms so the water will not go on the windows or house. I have struggled and struggled with that. Early this week Quentin said, "Turn the arms down."

It works great! I wanted to say, "Why in the hell didn't you tell me that all the times you fussed about the water on the side of the house and the windows?" I didn't though. I thanked him and bragged on him for being so smart.

If I were able to, I sure wouldn't have any trouble keeping busy. They are celebrating the Santa Fe Trail in Kansas this week. There was such an interesting program over at Maxwell Lake with a barbecue supper afterwards. Tonight they are at a place in Elyria. When the program is over people can take a walking trip where the wagon wheel ruts are still visible. There are some trail markers that are 175 years old. Tomorrow evening they will be in Lindsborg, the next evening at Windom, and they will keep moving west. It seems that there is something interesting going on a great deal of the time.

Your dad seems to be walking so much better. I think the water walking is helping him a lot. I have fussed with him so much about not walking on his toe. I've told him every few steps to walk flat and to put the right foot out in front of the left one. He practices that in the water, and I think it is getting to the place where he is remembering it. I'm very pleased about that.

He said the other night, "I'm living for Elaine to get here." He also said, "I know she can't do anything, but it will just be great to see her." I agree with him.

I'm hoping in the fall we could fly to see you. With Quentin being pretty much in control of his urination, it will make it possible for us to get away from home. I would make arrangements for a wheelchair for him to get around at the airport. I haven't said anything to him about it yet, but have hopes we can do that someday.

I'm enclosing a picture of Liz Taylor. Years and years ago I must have been fussing about my looks and apparently Quentin asked who I would like to look like. I can't remember the conversation. However, when I said, knowing it was impossible, that I would like to look like Liz Taylor,

Quentin said, "Oh, hell! You're better looking than she is."

It didn't change my opinion of myself, but it was always a source of amusement to me. When I saw the enclosed picture on the newsstand, I had to buy it. I feel that I am finally prettier than Liz Taylor! I have to look pretty hard for sources of fun, but I've laughed to myself thinking if someone asked you what your mother looked like, you could say, "She's better looking than Liz Taylor."

I do have some great thoughts at times. I told you about my friend saying she didn't have any fun. My first reaction was, "You ought to change places with me!"

As I got to thinking of the things I consider fun now, I consider your visits or visits from any of the family fun. It is great fun now to watch our great-grand-children grow and develop. It is fun to take the wonderful feeling warm dough out of a bowl to make rolls or delicious bread. It is fun to watch the grass and flowers develop. I had a lot of "fun" thinking about the fun things in my life and was amazed at how many things came to my mind.

I've been thinking about writing an article for our church paper. It might encourage a lot of the old people in our church to look at their own situation and see that they aren't completely bereft of fun. In the past, it has been fairly easy to graduate from one stage of fun to another. As a person reaches this stage, it is harder to give up those former stages. We still remember dancing, playing golf, traveling, etc. We now reluctantly accept that as the past. It is especially hard for Quentin to give up everything when he has so little to replace it.

I don't know what we will do for fun if it stays this hot when you come. Guess we will have to get up and out early in the morning. Right now, I'm planning on going over to Maxwell Game Preserve very early. We'll pack our breakfast and take the tour before the temperature gets up over 100.

Quentin got your beautiful Father's Day card and cried. He does that quite easily now at something touching or beautiful. Thank you very much.

We're sure looking forward to your visit. Can frequent flier miles be transferred? I have an AT&T True Rewards card. I would be glad to give them to you.

Tuesday AM

We went to town for blood tests and then to a restaurant for breakfast.

I had a biscuit with sausage gravy, which was delicious. Quentin had the combo – two pancakes, bacon and one egg. We each had coffee. It came to $7.06. I told the waitress I could fix breakfast at home for two weeks for that price – and have orange juice too!

You are probably running out of time, so I'll quit. The nice thing about writing letters is that a person has a captive audience, and one can ramble on and on without seeing a bored expression or being interrupted by someone who thinks he/she has something more interesting to say.

I'll look forward to talking on the phone.

Lots of love,

Mom

September 24, 1996

Dear Elaine and Alex,

I just realized a little while ago that I had missed a very important event today. It is the 25th anniversary of the Meals on Wheels program. Every year there is a coffee to thank the volunteers. I had it written on my calendar and just plain forgot. I think my thinking process is all messed up and filled up with Candi's new baby. It's a wonder I didn't come to about next Monday and remember that you had gotten married on Saturday.

Quentin fell again this evening. I was in the living room and heard a big crash, so I ran out to the dining room. I had to call Larry to come get him up. He evidently has wonderful bones – nothing seems to be broken. His walking ability is much better, but his speech is terrible. I don't know if it is my ears or if he is so much worse. I have a terrible time understanding him. He has a hard time getting his ideas out. I haven't said anything to him (it would really depress him) but I can't help but wonder if he didn't have a small stroke when he was so sick about three weeks ago.

We have not gone to the Y since they have gone back to the morning schedule. We really liked the 3:00 to 5:30 pm schedule during the summer. They adjust our time around the school kids. I commented to Quentin the other day that we just had to go back. He said he didn't want to try until after harvest. I asked why that should make a difference to us. He said, "I want to help with the harvest."

When I asked what he was going to do, he said he didn't know for sure, but he was going to help. I decided to let nature and Larry handle this one.

We have had so much fun watching the Monarch butterflies this past week. They seem to be gone today. They are migrating from Canada to Mexico. There was an article in the paper that said they only live two years, but they make this trip twice. They have a record of one tagged butterfly that traveled 1800 miles. The yard was full of them. They loved the butterfly bushes. When we looked out the window it appeared those bushes had a new kind of blossom on them. Once I looked out and saw the trees along the old feed bunk completely covered. I could have sat and watched them for hours.

It's a good thing that you are a strong person, Elaine.

With starting a new job, getting your house ready to sell, rearranging Alex's house to make room for you and Annie, and planning a wedding – a lot of people would be in bad shape emotionally. I'm very happy that you can handle stress.

I'm going to be eager to get your wedding pictures and hear about your meal and everything. It sounds as if you are going to have a beautiful, memorable day. Marg asked if it was going to be a big wedding. I said, "No," and then I thought with your three kids, Alex's five children, their spouses and his six grandkids that it won't be all that small. Annie said last night she was so excited about being your maid of honor that she was about to split. She also said Eric and Robert are happy about walking you down the aisle. I'm sure they'll look very handsome in their tuxedos.

I can understand why you thought eloping was a good idea, but I think Alex was wise to want a ceremony and to include all the kids and grandkids. I think it's also smart that you're getting married in Santa Fe, especially since none of his kids have been to your church in Albuquerque since their mother's funeral.

We wish we could be there, but have no regrets about our decision. We want you to be focusing on your happy occasion, not worrying about us. You both know we are wishing you the very best – and that is what we expect for you.

Lots of love,

Mom

October 28, 1996

Dear Elaine and Alex,

It was so good to talk to you last night. I had vicariously enjoyed your cruise. I was concerned that it would be a little calm for you. When you said the first two days at sea were wasted – I think you just needed the time to slow down. It was like Quentin when the fall work was done; he was still in high gear and it took a while for him to come down from the tension he had been under.

I remember one year when he followed me every place. When we were getting ready to go to town, he would follow me back and forth from the bedroom to the bathroom. When I was putting on my makeup, he just stayed and watched. I knew what his problem was and was glad when he was a normal, properly functioning human being again. I heard a program on TV not long ago talking about tension. They said even people who enjoyed their lives experienced a physical result of tension in their bodies.

I'm sure glad you and Alex are walking every morning. The remedy they prescribed on the TV show was some kind of physical activity. I think you two are doing fine. You both have such big jobs. I'm glad you had the experience at Univision – you met such interesting people – but I can understand how you couldn't turn down the offer from the CBS station. I know you didn't like it when they said you couldn't be promoted to General Manager at Univision because you weren't Hispanic. You've never really liked anyone putting limits on you, and it would be hard to not accept such a huge increase in salary.

Quentin worries about Alex working too hard. We can't imagine a school with 50,000 students. The whole population of Hutchinson is only 40,000. We just hope you won't work so hard that you forget to take time to enjoy each other.

You asked how I was feeling. Frankly, I guess I have to say I've felt lousy. Usually by 10:30 in the morning I feel so tired that I have to go back to bed. I don't have any alarming physical symptoms, but I have diagnosed my problem as depression. I was writing to Jean and telling her about it and I began to wonder if it wasn't just a bad case of self-pity. The flowers are dying and the prospect of winter doesn't thrill me at all.

I'm having a terrible time doing the most basic household jobs. I decided the other day the trouble is that I don't have a single thing to do that I want to do. I would probably feel better if I could force myself to get in gear and clean out the closets and cupboards and get everything in order. It seems like there is no end to it.

It will be three years on October 30 since Quentin had the stroke. It has been a case of taking one step forward and three back all the time. He is doing better except in his speech. It could be my ears, but I have a terrible time understanding him. It has been like that ever since he was so sick and constipated several weeks ago. After everything was over I wondered if he had experienced a mini-stroke.

He wants to do things so bad to help me. Quite often he thinks he can do something. My first reaction is to tell him he can't, and then I think he should be able to try. Sometimes he can and other times he can't. The other day he wanted to go out and put fertilizer on the yard. There was a big tree limb that had come down. He tried to move it to the dump, but just got to the corner of the garage before he wore out. He had to sit on the back steps to rest before he could even come in the house.

I am not getting enough sleep. Almost as soon as I lay down my legs start jumping. We start to bed by 10:00 pm and it is usually 1:00 or 2:00 before I get to sleep, and then I'm up several times in the night. The other night I had just gone to sleep when Quentin awakened me. He had rolled out of bed. He was flat on his back. I tried to get him in a sitting position, but every time we got close he would fall back down.

I got the bar off the hoist, got the belt on him and started to lift him. The electrical cord that went into the hoist became disconnected because it was lowered to its limit. The only way I could get it back in was to stand on the bed, which was very wiggly. I hooked it in, but I knew it hadn't gone in as far as it should have. I got down, hooked Quentin up again and the same thing happened all over again. The whole process took over an hour.

We went back to bed, and Quentin wanted me to lay next to him as he had gotten cold on the floor. I wasn't excited about that, but I didn't feel like getting out of bed to get him another cover. He moves so much that I can't stand to be next to him for very long. His motion usually gets me wide-awake, and then my legs start hurting. I finally got him another cover, and then I tried to get back to sleep again. I got up at 6:00 and went in on the living room floor and slept for two hours. I was so tired the next day I was literally sick.

Quentin has been so worried about me, and I hate to do that to him, but there is no way I can conceal how I feel when I can hardly get around. When I think there isn't anything I like to do, I am brought up short thinking about all he has had to give up. He has had his time of depression, and I have never been critical of it.

We were talking the other day about events leading up to the stroke. I said it was like a TV picture just before a rocket lift off. This would be in days, marking the events with each day one closer to the catastrophe. Quentin had been talking about taking an Alaskan cruise the next summer, and I was already getting a few things together to go to Florida in January. And then on October 30, the big explosion happens!

I hated to tell you how I was feeling, but I remember the time you scolded me for not telling you about the lupus. I really don't expect anything terrible when I go to the doctor, but felt you should probably be prepared in case there is a problem.

Thank you for sending the wedding photos. All of the kids looked so beautiful and so handsome. We have just about looked the pictures off. You and Alex looked great. We loved your dress. I think the planning was perfect. It seemed like an awful lot of work for the short time it took (the tired old mom again) but I think it was wonderful. We loved hearing all about it, but didn't have any feeling of regretting we hadn't gone. It would have been too much work and worry for you to have us there.

I told Quentin I had to start getting ready for you and Alex. Now I just have to clean the green hairy stuff out of the refrigerator, knock down the cobwebs we've been dodging, pick up the dirty clothes off the chairs, and we will be in pretty good shape. I'm going to start getting some things ready so that food will not be a problem.

I don't want to ask Teri to have Thanksgiving dinner. Her dad has another lump on his throat and is going in for a biopsy next week. I told Greg and Deb you were coming and invited them. I also invited Gene and Gloria.

It is going to be simple, though. I said last year after Thanksgiving that was the last mashed potatoes and gravy dinner I was fixing, but I don't want to eat out. I can't imagine Thanksgiving without leftovers. Besides, we'll have fun working together in the kitchen.

Lots of love,

Madelyn

November 9, 1996

Dear Elaine and Alex,

We have been thinking about you and Alex a lot today. I made your motel reservation. It's in the Courtyard – upstairs in a non-smoking room. I was amused when I called in. At first she didn't think she had anything. She asked for the name and address. She suddenly found this room with a king size bed when I told her it was for Dr. and Mrs. Alex Sanchez. Guess she was properly impressed with your desirability as a guest.

I got my refrigerator cleaned up real well last week. I got started on the cupboards today. I had everything in excellent shape when Jean and Frank came in March. I haven't touched the cupboards since. As much as I enjoy clean cupboards, it would seem that I would do it more often.

The drug I'm taking for sleep is continuing to be effective. I have gotten over my depression and have a lot more energy. The doctor prescribed a new nose sprayer for Quentin, and it is helping him.

We are very excited about your coming. I'm counting the days. It will only be nine! As fast as time goes, it will be here before we know it.

I know you are very happy and life is good for you now, but I still have to say I wish you a happy birthday and a great year!

Love,

Mom

December 4, 1996

Dear Elaine and Alex,

We just wanted to tell you again how very much we enjoyed your visit. We also thank you for the "boom box." We both love it! I went to the library yesterday and checked out some CD's. I'm playing one now that is Johann Strauss favorites. It is beautiful. Last night we played a Unity tape that turned out to be just what we needed to hear.

I wrote a letter to the whole family on Sunday evening and then decided to not send it. I had a brain scan and a carotid artery Doppler on Monday. I knew the Tuesday before Thanksgiving that I was going to have it done, but I didn't say anything to anyone – not even Quentin. I had been feeling like I was going to fall. I had an experience on Monday night, a week ago, that caused me to call the doctor.

I have decided I was probably having a reaction to drugs. My legs were just awful that night, and I couldn't get them straightened out. I took the medication the doctor prescribed, and when I got up to go to bed I could hardly walk. I started seeing diamond shaped "things." I had trouble finding the bed and getting on it. When I finally did get in bed I was seeing multiple diamond shaped things in various colors.

I was smart enough that I remembered all of the covers on the bed were solid. My legs still wouldn't settle down, so I got up again and went to the living room. I was standing by my La-Z-Boy, and I saw a lot of wires above the chair. I reached up to touch them, but there wasn't anything there. I finally got over that nightmare and went to sleep, but I could hardly navigate the next day.

I called the doctor's office the next morning and got right in. They took three vials of blood and checked for a lot of things. They gave me instructions for some other tests, but I couldn't get them done until Monday. I started using my good old Unity affirmations, which have been a help before, and I began to feel much better. I only had a minimum amount of dizziness. Quentin was very concerned.

That evening I told him I thought the falling feeling

was probably coming from my ears. I was afraid he would get started crying, but he never did. I tried to assure him that the test would come out alright. That is when we listened to the Unity tape. It sounded as if it had been made for us. Yesterday the doctor called to tell me that everything was fine. I had given him instructions that he was not to find any tumors or Alzheimer's disease. I did give him permission to find something simple that could be taken care of with a pill. Next time I see him at the hospital, I will tell him he "done good."

Quentin and I have had some good heart to heart visits since he found out about this. He is doing his bike riding without having to be told. So that's good. It came up that we'd be in a hell of a mess if I got sick or had to have surgery. I told him the only alternative would be for him to go to a nursing home until I was able to take care of him again.

He informed me that he wouldn't go and that he would stay right here. I reminded him he couldn't live by himself, and he responded by saying he would sure give it a try. I have been interested to see that he is doing more for himself. I was terribly tired this morning and didn't wake up when he got up. When I did get up, Quentin was dressed. He had even taken a clean shirt out of the closet for himself.

Frank called Monday night to say that Jean was in the

hospital. She got up at 6:00 am to go to the bathroom. She fell and broke her leg. The doctor showed them the X-rays. Frank said her bone looked like a broken windshield. She will be sent to a rehab hospital for three weeks. She said that would sure beat having Frank take care of her. She also said they would be pulling each others' hair out if he had to take care of her during the convalescence.

Well, Quentin wants to start getting ready for bed. I was so tired last night I didn't pound my legs. I had to get up and do it, as they started jumping. We thank you for that gift, too. That little gadget seems to help when I use it. I am also using the perfume lavishly, as you suggested, and I enjoy it very much.

Lots of love,

Mom

Chapter 4 - 1997

January 11, 1997

Dear Elaine and Alex,

When I called Time and Temperature this morning it was minus one. I have plenty of food on hand to sustain us during a bad siege. I just hope the electricity stays on.

Quentin and I stopped at Braums to eat the other evening, and he fell. He skinned up his left knee and broke a lot of fingernails, but otherwise was not hurt. There were four Japanese boys sitting at a table close to our booth. Two of them jumped up and came to help him get up. There were a couple cowboy-type men there, and as soon as we were ready to leave, they came to ask if they could help. They followed us out to the car.

We are constantly amazed at how good people have been. There are lots of people who complain about being treated bad because of their age or disabilities. We have never encountered anything except respect and wonderful treatment.

I'm going to Hutchinson Wednesday for a free ear test. I would guess the free test makes you feel like you can't live without their product. The hearing product is called "Nu-Ear Microscoptics." I dread to think of what it might cost. The Miracle Ear was $1,100 several years ago.

I was thrilled with the comments your general

manager made to you. It is sure nice that they are encouraging you with their good opinions while you are having to make so many tough decisions and changes.

Your father will be 78 next week. That seems incredible to me! We were very active in American Agriculture when Quentin was 60 years old. We were working with so many young people, and we didn't feel older than any of them. Quentin was a good-going concern for almost 15 years after that.

Well, maybe I will have something interesting to talk about next time – let's hope so. Hope you are both enjoying your work and your life.

Lots of love,

Mom

January 17, 1997

Dear Elaine and Alex,

There really isn't anything very exciting or interesting to talk about. It has been cold, cold and cold. It was seven years ago today that I had the heart surgery. It sure doesn't seem as if it were that long ago. I'm glad that the recovery period is over. I'm grateful Quentin was still well at that time.

I ordered a pair of new hearing aids and now I've been worrying myself silly about it. They are horribly expensive. I guess I'm not being extravagant, but it sure is hard to spend the money.

I went to coffee with those interesting women again last week. The entire conversation was on books and things in the news. I was most impressed with them again. I sat and read the *Time Magazine* from cover to cover the day it came this week so I could keep up. I have given up watching television news because I can't understand a word that is being said.

I understand my mother much better now that my hearing has deteriorated. She very seldom turned on her TV, and she wouldn't go to the Bible classes when she lived at the Cedars. One day Laura Hill told her that a Christian Church minister was leading the lesson. Mother responded by saying, "I wouldn't go if Jesus Christ himself was giving the lesson."

When a person can't hear, it gets to the place where you really don't want to be around people. There have been times when I have said to myself, "I would pay any price to be able to hear well." I think I just have, so we will see.

Herb Smith called yesterday from the college to tell me how much his students had loved my presentation on Unity. That perked me up right away. He said they liked my bearing and the presentation. He was surprised when I told him I felt like I had fallen flat. Young people can be absolutely expressionless, which can throw me. They were so informal. I was scared before I ever started, and I thought they looked bored. I'm glad to know they liked it.

I will be very eager to hear about Alex's college board election in February. I can't blame him for not wanting to put up with the constant problems caused by some of his board members. We will pray that the right decisions are made, whichever way it goes. It is no doubt a good feeling to know that you are in a financial position where you don't have to take whatever they dish out. I personally feel it will be a great loss to the school if you decide to go.

It is past time for lunch, and the mailman will be going soon, so will say so long.

Lots of love,

Madelyn

March 19, 1997

Dear Elaine and Alex,

I have had a wonderful experience which I wanted to share with you. I have a feeling you might have been responsible for it. I remember telling you all the little things about Quentin that were irritating me so. About two weeks ago I realized I wasn't having that problem any more. His actions had not changed – but my reaction had. I felt as if you had been praying for me. In case it wasn't you, it could have been in response to the prayer I say every night in which I ask that we will learn the lessons that are here to be learned. It has taken a lot of pressure off me.

Jean and Frank are coming on May 6. I wrote and told her that I was in a much better emotional state now than when they came last year. I told her I was just about at the end of my rope then, but I have learned how to tie a knot and hang on. I do look forward to seeing them. Frank watches after Quentin so Jean and I can get away.

Quentin has been fussing about my being gone so much. After I talked to you last night and told him that you said you and Alex had been talking, he said, "I wish you would sit and talk with me."

My life is not real inclusive. When I'm on the computer there is no place for him. Same thing when I do the bookkeeping. I forgot to tell you I was so frustrated on the last day of my computer class that I felt like I was going to go into a kicking, crying, screaming fit. As I was walking out the door Quentin was so sincere when he said, "I am so sorry."

Last summer our minister commented that Quentin was sure lucky to have me. My reply was, "I have been lucky to have him all these years." When he is irritating I know he is not doing it deliberately, and that he would much prefer to not be doing the irritating things. Glad my heart and head have gotten together on that.

I went through a terrible time for two or three years after our old people died. I was real paranoid about getting old after looking after Grandpa Stan and my folks. I finally realized with God's help I had been able to get through some very unpleasant experiences, and that God would be there for me through old age.

I have come to the conclusion – or the understanding – that a person gets what he thinks about. The Apostle Paul made the statement, "What I have feared has come upon me."

I was telling Quentin that one day, and of course, he didn't agree with me. I had often said if I had a heart attack I didn't want anyone to try to rescue me. Quentin used to tell me if he had a stroke he wanted me to go off and leave him. I was to come back in an hour to check on him, and if he were still alive I was to go away again. Guess who had heart surgery and who had a stroke.

When Quentin had the stroke he didn't fuss about going to the hospital. He still complains to me that if I would have left him alone when he developed pneumonia instead of calling an ambulance that he would have died. (He didn't complain about going to the hospital at that time either.)

I guess the lesson is to be selective in the things you choose to think about.

Love,

Mom

March 24, 1997

Dear Elaine and Alex,

We just received the letter and brochure from you. I'm really impressed with all your accomplishments, Alex! You have had a busy, worthwhile life. It would be a pleasure to know you even if we weren't lucky enough to have you for a son-in-law. Of course, just being what you are as an individual makes you completely acceptable.

Quentin went to church with me yesterday morning. I'm always happy when he feels like going. It is quite an ordeal to get him ready, and I can't go down for coffee when he goes. I miss that, but I'm willing to give it up. He needs to get out more.

I had an appointment in Hutchinson last Thursday to have my hearing aids checked. I didn't want Quentin to go, but I didn't want to tell him that I didn't want him. I reminded him that I wanted to do some shopping and that would mean a lot of sitting in the car for him, to which he said, "That would be all right." I decided to try another track, so I said very cheerfully that we could eat our lunch out if he went with me.

By the time we got to Anthony's he was gasping for breath. The only chairs were at the back of the shoe department, but there was a ledge on the window, so the clerk told him to sit there. I didn't see anything I liked so we made a slow procession across the street to the car.

We drove to Pegues next. He could have gone into their coffee shop and waited for me, but he wouldn't do that. He wanted to be by my side. I looked, but couldn't concentrate on anything, so we left again.

We stopped at Wal-Mart to see if they had anything in the Kathie Lee line. I took three pairs of size 10 pants to the dressing room, and they were all way too big. Since there was no clerk to take the big ones and bring the small ones, I put on my other clothes and we left.

When we got to the Precision Hearing Aid Center I wanted Quentin to go in and use the restroom. He wouldn't do that. When I got back out to the car, I said, "Well, now we will go for lunch."

He informed me in no uncertain terms that he wanted to go home. I informed him in no uncertain terms that the deal was we would eat lunch out. I refrained from telling him he had ruined my morning, and I was at least going to get lunch out of it.

We went to the Amarillo Grill and Bar, and he went to the restroom, which is at the very back of the building. He did take the cane (reluctantly). We got back to the restroom, and I was waiting for him in the hall when I heard a lot of pounding on the restroom wall. It didn't take long to figure out that he had fallen. I opened the door and could see he was in such a position that he couldn't get up and I couldn't get in.

I hurried to get the manager, but he wasn't up at the front as he usually is. I told a waitress, and she went rushing after him. He came running to the restroom right away. He got Quentin up and then politely came out into the hall and waited with me. Pretty soon he suggested I go to our table, which was ready, and he said he would bring Quentin in. We had the nicest waitress and a good lunch.

A couple nights before that, I had been up at 12:30 doing exercises, as my legs were bothering me. I heard him get out of bed, and pretty soon I heard a familiar thump. Three nights in the previous ten days he rolled out of bed. He sleeps precariously close to the edge of the bed and rolls out. I guess you could classify those as the exciting events in our daily routine.

I was thrilled yesterday to discover little tiny leaves coming from the roots of the roses the rabbits had eaten. I thought they were completely dead. Also, the butterfly bushes show signs of having life, and I thought they were gone. I had thought that I really wasn't interested in the process of doing the flowers this year, but I find that I am. I was also thrilled to find yesterday that I have a lot more energy and stamina than I have had for a long time.

I have to get some things in the mail for the bank so had better move along. Would much rather "talk" to you. It is such a joy to us to know that everything is going so well for you.

Love you,

Mom

133

April 8, 1997

Dear Elaine and Alex,

Have been getting compliments from Quentin several times a day recently. That is thanks to a pair of size 8 petite jeans I purchased at Wal-Mart. Can you believe it! If I refer to your little, white-haired mother, it will be the truth.

I have been wanting to tell you how beautiful the pear trees have been this spring. The blossoms are starting to turn into leaves now. The little tree you gave me for Mother's Day two or three years ago has a lot of flowers on it. It is interesting. They aren't very large, but they are spaced much like a gladioli. We have enjoyed that.

We are still enjoying watching the birds. I was telling Jean that we've had a red bird visiting recently. She said it was a Cardinal, the state bird of Virginia. You are supposed to put your hand over your heart when you see one. Quentin can sit and watch the birds for hours. I'm still amazed the feeder stays perfectly clean. They aren't so careful in the birdbath.

Lots of Love,

Mom

April 15, 1997

Dear Elaine and Alex

I mentioned in the last letter how pretty the trees were. Well, we had much below freezing weather, and it sure took care of the beautiful flowering trees. They look pathetic. Larry said he thought the tree damage was cosmetic. He thinks they'll come out of it. He feels the same way about the wheat.

Your vacation time is approaching rapidly. I checked out an Irving Stone book recently, *The Greek Treasure*, and have read some of it. He weaves a good story based on facts, letters, etc. We anticipate seeing your pictures and hearing of your experiences.

I'm so glad all of your kids are doing so well. I'm wondering if they have found a house suitable for the three of them. I'm sure Annie is getting eager to graduate and get out on her own.

Must run! Hope everything is well with both of you.

Lots of love,

Mom

May 14, 1997

Dear Elaine and Alex

Jean and Frank left this morning. We sure enjoyed their visit. Frank would insist on taking care of Quentin and told Jean and I to go off and do something – which we did every day! We ate lunch at home only two days during the time they were here. Frank was feeling pretty good, and he likes to be busy, so he did a lot around here.

We are certainly anticipating your visit. After you

folks leave we won't have anything to anticipate for a long time. As Joe Straka used to say, "Mom and I just sit around and look mean at each other."

I had fun with some plants last week. I took one to town to give to my friend Gladys. She wasn't home, so I watered the plant good and put it in an empty planter on the porch. It didn't show much, so I was going to call and tell her about it, but I forgot. On Monday Jean and I were in town, so I went by the Naylor's house to see if they had come home. They hadn't, but the plant had grown so much that it was very visible. I watered it again and left. I called that evening. They had just been home an hour. They had seen the plant but had no idea who it was from. That was fun.

Had already addressed this letter and had it in an envelope before I went to get the mail. The scarf and your card came. <u>I love the scarf!</u> Don't think there will a lot of them in McPherson. Maybe it's my imagination, but you said you bought it in the Spice Market in Istanbul. It seems to me to have a spicy fragrance.

The card was beautiful. It made your dad cry. I could have. It means a lot to me to get such cards. I have always regretted that I could not send a card to my mother. I used to stand in front of card racks and cry when I read such sentiments. I always felt guilty because I didn't feel love for my mother. I remember being disappointed when

I was told she'd be coming home from the hospital with my new baby sister. I was excited about the baby, but I didn't want Mother to come home. Even at three, I knew that was wrong.

Well, enough of that. Thanks a million for the beautiful Mother's Day gift!

Lots of love,

Mom

May 16, 1997

Dear Annie,

Wish we could be there for your graduation. You have probably heard that Grandpa has a motorized scooter now, so he's getting around so much better. We will get the lift next week, and that will be wonderful. Maybe we can travel again soon.

I can't help thinking how wonderful it is to be a young woman graduating from high school now. I loved high school. One day shortly after I graduated, I was on my hands and knees washing the dining room floor for my mother and I had the thought, "I could do this for other people and earn my room and board to go to school."

At that time we lived in a little town, and I had a job with the superintendent of schools for the fabulous sum of $50 a month. My folks thought it was great that I could live at home and make all that money. They were very opposed to me going to school! My dad finished the fifth grade, and my mother finished the eighth grade, so they thought a high school degree was a big deal and enough education for any woman; but I had bigger dreams and more ambition than that. I got a cash scholarship to a business school in Wichita and a job in the school's office.

Christy cried for days before she left for college. She was afraid to leave home! I had said goodbye to her a few days before she left. If I would have gone over the day she left I would probably have cried too! I usually say I don't want to go back and relive yesterday, but I would have sold my soul to the devil that day to be eighteen years old and going to college.

I never was afraid of anything. My dad told me once that he worried about me because nothing scared me. (My mother was afraid of everything – especially anything electrical.) When I went to Tacoma, Washington to be married, I was standing on a hill one day and could see town any direction I looked. I was so thrilled – that big place and I didn't know a soul. The whole city was there for me to conquer.

At one time I had a very responsible job. I was the general manager of three grain elevators and a feed mill. I got the promotion from office manager to general manager after my boss committed suicide. They never got his blood out of the cracks in the linoleum under my desk (where he'd shot himself). I used to think about him not being able to handle the pressure of the job. When he went home his wife served him a cocktail and dinner. When I went home I changed clothes and went to the milk barn.

We always had Thanksgiving and Christmas with Marg and Dale. One particular Thanksgiving Marg and I were doing dishes. I commented that I thought every girl should be required to take typing and bookkeeping before graduating. Marg had a fit. She said, "You think everyone should be a career woman. You don't think it is important to be a housewife."

I very calmly explained that I had known so many women who had stayed in terrible marriages because they had no training and no way of supporting themselves. Also, a person never knows when a situation comes up where it would be imperative for the woman to work. I have used my typing and bookkeeping ability right here on the farm, and I get a lot of pleasure out of being able to use the computer. I still like going to school. A few years ago I drove to Hutch to take a basic accounting course. This past winter I took a course in WordPerfect. I can't say that I enjoyed that, but I am glad to have the knowledge and ability to use what I mastered.

It is very exciting to realize that if a person has a good mind there is no age limit to continue learning and growing. The days aren't long enough for me to master all the things I'm interested in, and there are probably not enough years left to do everything I want to do.

I will be very interested in hearing of your progress and decisions. You have a lot going for you. You are healthy and intelligent and have numerous talents. You will be backed wholeheartedly in a decision to get some education.

It is impossible at this stage of life to know absolutely for sure what you want to do. You have no idea how things will unfold for you. Your mother at one time expected to spend her life on the farm. She had no concept of the ability she had. She never even dreamed of getting to travel as much as she has. You live each day to the best of your ability and keep an open mind. We are wishing you the very best for now and always.

Lots of love,

Grandma

June 10, 1997

Dear Elaine and Alex,

It is a very pleasant day. I have watered everything real good and Quentin is mowing the Courtyard. When he is mowing the yard I experience a great deal of stress. It is interesting how acute my hearing is when he is out mowing by himself.

A week ago he was out in the old cow lot, and I realized I didn't hear the mower. I hurried out to check on him. I didn't see the mower anyplace. I decided he might have taken it up to the shop for some reason or the other and was about to go in, but I still didn't feel satisfied. I walked a little farther, and my heart nearly stopped when I saw the front end of the mower sticking up on the edge of the lagoon (known as the poopy pond around here) and there was no operator in sight.

In just a little bit I saw Quentin struggling to stand up. I still haven't figured out why he was mowing in that particular location. It was obviously muddy. There is a mound of dirt around it, which he was mowing, and the machine started spinning. He can't get off by himself under the best of conditions, so he had to roll off. He told me to go get the pickup and a chain so we could pull it out.

I didn't say so, but I was thinking *we* were not going to pull it out. I found Larry, and as soon as I told him the situation, he told his two nephews to get a chain and a four-wheeler and come down and take care of it. We sat and watched them, and they had quite a time. I thought they were going to have to go after a tractor, but they finally got it out. Fortunately, none of the working parts of the mower had been submerged.

Last week we went to the Health-Equip store in Hutchinson for another lesson on loading and unloading the scooter. We're doing much better with it. It has given us tremendous freedom to go places.

I have figured out a wonderful plan for both of you. Turn in your resignations, purchase a motor home and travel for a year seeing scenery and looking at different job opportunities. This is something I always wanted to do.

I didn't sleep much last night after talking with you—thinking about stress—not only about you folks but about me. I have been reading Deepak Chopra's book, *Ageless Body, Timeless Mind.* At one place in the main chapter on stress he made the following statement: Everyone has a different level of stress tolerance, but what seems to produce the greatest perceived threat in a given situation are the following:

Lack of predictability

Lack of control

Lack of outlets for frustration

Is that food for thought – or what? There is so much more, but I can't print the whole book. Underneath the title is an interesting description. It is: *The Quantum Alternative to Growing Old.*

I'm on the second time around of reading out loud *The Quest - a Spiritual Journey*, which is a rather new Unity textbook. Typically, if Quentin doesn't like the statements made in a book, he will say he doesn't agree with them. He implies that he is right and the authors are wrong. I never feel I have to accept everything as being 100% right, but I do like to keep an open mind.

I had started a chapter on love last night. The author stated that love is already present in us in the form of God. Our job is to release that love. So many stories are told about how babies who are failing in orphanages improve when they are loved. The author said when the babies were rocked and cuddled they could release the love within themselves. That was an interesting line of thought, which tied in with other things. One very invigorating thought for me is that I can't possibly live long enough to learn all that I want to. It beats thinking that life is practically over and there is nothing to do.

Well, I want to get this in the mail tonight, and I'm going to have to hurry to get to town soon. Sure enjoyed talking to both of you this past week.

Hope all is well for both of you and all of your kids. I'm pleased that Annie is going to work for her Uncle Jim this summer. I knew a woman once who worked in a vet's office. I thought the best story was when she told about a person bringing in her constipated turtle! On this I will say goodbye and God bless.

Lots of love,

Madelyn

June 22, 1997

Dear Elaine and Alex,

We drove to Hays so we could show Quentin's scooter to our friend Ed Fellers. It was a beautiful drive. Everything was so lush and green. The wind was blowing very hard, and at one place I actually saw *waves of golden grain*! It was probably the direction we were driving, the position of the sun, and the way the wind was blowing.

Ed's legs have given out, and he has more trouble walking than Quentin does. He was not the least bit interested in the scooter. That surprised us. His mind is not as good as it used to be, and his personality is different. He used to tell one funny story after another. He was a strong individualist and a "good" man. His comment about the scooter was that it was probably like buying a Cadillac. (He has had several.)

That night Quentin said, "I had a terrible blow today." He said he would not go back unless it was for Ed's funeral. I commented that is how people feel when they come see him. Unfortunately, people do stay away when they see someone with physical problems that will not be overcome.

We have had two of the cutest little baby squirrels playing in our yard. However, the fact that they ate the leaves off of the impatiens took away from the pleasure of watching them. I read someplace to keep animals out of flowers beds that you should surround it with human urine. I went out this morning with the urinal and had enough to go all around the flower bed underneath the big hackberry tree on the south side of the house. I haven't seen any of the animals today, which is unusual. Maybe it worked.

The yellow rose I purchased with your Mother's Day money was eaten down to the roots, but is doing great now. It has five flowers on it. Quentin mowed over all the other roses. One bush was trying to make a comeback, but with being eaten by the varmints and getting mowed down twice, it had all the stress it could take.

I picked a big geranium bloom and put it in the little vase you sent from Greece. Marg came over yesterday to visit, and we were at the table having a glass of tea when she commented about it being such an interesting vase. I have planted a lot of red flowers so I'll always have something to put in it. We're enjoying it very much.

Quentin has gone to bed. He was feeling "down" tonight. I never know just what to say when he feels the way he did tonight. He feels he is useless. The harvest will start next week, and it is probably bothering him that he can't be part of it.

It is almost 11pm, so I had better sign off and get to bed. We're looking forward to hearing from you. The Father's Day card was beautiful. Quentin enjoyed the letter, even though it made him cry. That was a wonderful verse on the card.

Lots of love,

Madelyn

July 4, 1997

Dear Elaine and Alex,

I remember how much fun we had last year on the Fourth of July weekend. I told Quentin the other day that I wished you were here this year. He said, "You are just going to have to get used to it."

I am, and it has been just a little over a month since you were here, so I'm not feeling sorry for myself for not getting to see you. We received your letter and the check yesterday, and I thank you.

I'm feeling so good now! It is wonderful! Trying to remember when I had felt this good. There was one day a few years ago when I felt great until noon, and I was so thrilled. By noon it was gone.

Think the reason I am feeling so good is that I have learned to completely relax. I can rest for a short time and get up feeling great. Also, my friend, Deepak Chopra, said that we have a completely new skeleton every three years. I give thanks morning and night for the new atoms and cells and visualize them renewing my body according to God's original plan.

The harvest will be finished this evening. It started on Monday. Larry had both of our combines going and hired a custom cutter with three new John Deere cutters. The wheat has been wonderful. The lowest yield has been 71 bushels per acre. We have never had a harvest like that. We probably won't have any more money than we did last year, as instead of being $5, it is just a little over $3 a bushel.

On Wednesday our temperature was 107. Larry has been under a lot of stress, which he doesn't handle well. He had a truck driver tell him to go f___ himself the other day when they were unloading a truck of wheat in Conway. The driver was so mad he started walking home. Larry had to go apologize and get him back in the truck. That is not easy for him. He used to get disagreeable with Quentin, and if he got too bad, Quentin would leave.

Larry has started smoking again. He is gaining weight and his blood pressure is going up. Teri said she is worried that he'll have a stroke. I told her maybe he would be lucky and it would kill him. She really didn't want that. She said he was too young. Teri has told him she won't take care of him if he gets cancer. She would put him in a nursing home. I reminded her there was a little matter of money.

I have an appointment with the hearing aid man on Thursday so will try to see your boys. I was surprised they decided to come back to Hutchinson, but I know their experience in Albuquerque was a lot different from yours. When a person is at the bottom end of the pay scale, life can be much tougher. The cost of living in Hutch is a lot less, but the opportunities are certainly limited as well. I hope it works out for them.

I don't think Quentin is doing well. I have so much difficulty understanding him, and his walking is terrible. Have been putting the weights on his legs and then I lift them up and straighten his knees. I have him use his muscles to lower them. He complains about it hurting the muscles in the back of his leg, but he doesn't get any sympathy from me. He had been lifting his leg only a few inches and practically letting it drop. I have told him the purpose of the exercise was not to see how fast he could do it.

This will distress you – but it is the truth. I can't think of much I enjoy about living with him any more. We used to say spontaneously, "You are so much fun to live with!"…"I love living with you," etc., etc. We haven't either one said that since October 30, 1993.

He has never been able to spell very well, and I have come to the conclusion that in his mind love was spelled s-e-x. Between the stroke and the cancer shots that is a thing of the past. Thank goodness he isn't mean about it, as a lot of men are. I informed him a long time ago that I would not have any patience with that at all.

Saturday morning

We went to Sirloin Stockade for dinner last night. The steak was delicious. We didn't have the company, the atmosphere, or the drinks, so we didn't enjoy it as much as we did last year when we went with you and Gene and Gloria to the Hideaway in Lindsborg. We didn't get to go to the concert, as Quentin spilled chocolate syrup – lots of it down the front of his shirt and pants. He needs sideboards on his spoons to hold all he tries to put on. That is another one of the things I don't like.

Sure wish Quentin could get off chemotherapy every three months, as I don't think it is helping his general condition. Sure don't want the cancer to spread to any other part of his body though. The doctor takes a PSA test every three months. His was 0.6 last month, so that is quite an improvement over what it was at the beginning. Think it was 180.

Sure glad I got out the Dummies book and learned to number pages. That has been the easiest thing I have mastered. Enjoy Word Perfect more every day.

Love,

Mom

July 11, 1997

Dear Elaine and Alex,

I went to Hutchinson yesterday and stopped by Target to see your boys. While I was there I decided to check and see if they had a bed rail. I found one in the infant department. I struggled and struggled to get this simple item (according to the box) put together. There were times when I tried to enlist Quentin's help, but he is worse than no help. I'm hoping it will prevent him from rolling out of bed so much.

I also stopped at Precision Ear to have my hearing aid checked. I told the doctor I would be willing to give him back that little jewel for the right ear. I can hear better without it. I've had a miserable time understanding Quentin. It was terribly discouraging for him to have to repeat something two or three times and then have me guess what he was saying.

The technician said the hearing aid was full of wax, so he cleaned it out. I asked him if I should use ear drops or what I could do. He said to come in every three months and have them cleaned. If I start having trouble under-standing Quentin again, I'll make an appointment right away. It is hard to describe how wonderful it is to be hearing again.

Have had fun planning to have my prestigious group of women friends out here for coffee. This is my invitation:

Madelyn Kubin would enjoy having you as a Friday
Morning Coffee Guest
at Quin Lynn Farm
July 25
If it has not rained the previous night
Is not raining that morning, and
If the wind is not blowing
More than 30 MPH

I will serve a couple kinds of homemade rolls, bacon, cantaloupe and coffee. The sister-in-law of my bitchy friend Sadie will come on Friday morning. She is a lot of fun, and I like her real well. I mentioned recently that Sadie and I were not bosom friends. Also, I said that she was the most intelligent woman I've ever known when it comes to getting things done. I have always thought she should have been a congresswoman. She would teach those men a thing or two! We started exchanging some stories about her, and Norma Tucker spoke up and said there were two women in McPherson that she wouldn't want to get in a fight with – Sadie and me. She said we were both very powerful women.

I told her I had never thought of myself as being powerful. I'm certainly not manipulative like Sadie. After I thought about it, I told Norma I was going to take that as a compliment.

Had an interesting experience this week. One day Quentin got out the telephone directory. I asked what he was looking for. He said his garage door wouldn't open, and he was trying to find a company that worked on overhead doors. He never has been able to find anything in the Yellow Pages, so I offered to help. The only company listed was in Salina, and he told me to call them.

I would not have bothered Larry that day if Quentin had been on the floor in the garage. I suggested we wait, as it wasn't an emergency for him to be able to get the pickup out. He didn't want to wait and insisted I call. I told him it would be very expensive. He didn't care what it cost, I was to call. I made the call and set up an appointment for them to come.

That night it rained, so Larry came over to visit. I asked him to look at it. He crawled up on the back of the pickup, and in less than five minutes he had the garage opener working. The service call was going to be $37.50 plus mileage. Quentin was provoked that I had canceled the appointment and had asked Larry fix it. He said, "When you see clothes you want you sure don't have trouble spending the money."

That rankled! Finally he told me what had happened to the garage door. He had backed out while it was in the process of lifting, and he did not want to have to tell me about it. Yesterday afternoon it quit again, so I called the repair people this morning. They came out and put new metal strips on the track to stabilize it and oiled everything.

We are so thrilled you folks are coming over Labor Day. Quentin will be asking me every few days if that is the day you are coming. He is really confused now. I have invited the church group to come out this Wednesday, and the Coffee Group will be here on July 25. He has asked me any number of times if this was the day someone was coming. He wanted to know what date you were coming. I told him Labor Day was on September 1.

He said he thought that was the date of his class reunion. I assured him it was all right—the reunion is on August 1. He is trying to be extra careful so nothing happens to prevent his going to the reunion. He said last night he wanted to see if Avis had gotten fat. (She's the girl he took to his senior prom.)

Saturday

I'm so pleased with the bed rail. Checked on Quentin a couple times last night and he was well back from the edge of the bed. It can be lowered to the side so that the bed can be made and the spread put on. Best $14.95 I have ever spent!

Don't think I told you that Eric looked handsome and very mature. He wanted my telephone number, which pleased me. Told him I loved company and would be glad to fix him a meal but would need a little advance notice. He has had a promotion, but Robert's didn't come through. He said there is another opening going to be available very soon and that Robert will get it. The kids all seem to have a good work ethic, which is good. I think they have done very well with every job they've ever had. I still marvel at Eric taking pride in being such a good dishwasher. He undoubtedly learned a lot there.

Thought you might like a few hints about your Christmas present. There is no way money can buy it, and it is almost irreplaceable. If you should guess, I will let you open it much sooner.

Lots of love,

Mom

July 16, 1997

Dear Family,

Our Church Fellowship has a carry-in luncheon once a month. I decided I would have them come to the farm this time, and have had more fun getting ready for them. Except for being a little windy, it was a perfect morning. I sprayed the yard with Yard Guard and there wasn't a fly or mosquito in sight. There were 24 of us.

Quentin was there and he enjoyed himself so much. He was sitting with some especially interesting people. I regret I didn't get a picture of him with the happy expression he had on his face. It is something that triggers memories of the past, but it is very rare now. The experience is somewhat like the feeling one has playing golf – one good shot makes a person want to go back and try for it again. I will be trying to think of things for him to do so I can see that expression again.

There was a section in the paper today about the County Fair at Canton which starts Friday. I don't think Quentin and I have been there together since we were dating and attended the street dance in the evening. Quentin commented that we could go this year. I took him up on that immediately!

They have a free buffalo feed Friday and a rodeo afterwards. I said we should go that night. His response was, "Isn't that the night of the reunion?"

I have told him at least 25 times that the reunion is on August 1. He wants to go see one person – Avis, his old heartthrob.

After thinking about Norma's comment about me being a powerful woman, I informed Teri and Larry that the trash pit has been a sore spot to me all these years. I hate to look out the kitchen window and see it, and I always hate to have guests see it. I'm calling Roland Johnson today. I'm going to tell him to bring his maintainer and come cover it up.

I also informed anyone who was in hearing distance

that I wanted the small grain bin emptied of all the barrels and my old ironer. Will have a door put on it and have it painted. It will be a place to store hoses and lawn furniture. Can hardly wait to find someplace else to show my power!

I'm going to start keeping a daily journal of our experiences with the idea in mind that I might eventually put it all into a book. I think it might help other people who are struggling with a handicapped person cope with their situations.

At the very beginning of this ordeal I prayed I would be willing to be a channel for God's love and caring. There were lots of times when I felt I was really being "used" in a good manner. There also have been many times when I forget I am serving God, and I am very conscious that Madelyn is really not enjoying this experience. There are even times when I feel like telling God I want to play something else, and he should find himself another servant! I always feel guilty and ask forgiveness and go back to handling the situation in an acceptable way.

One more hint about your Christmas present. You might like to know that it won't fade, shrink or go out of style.

Lots of love,

Mom

July 28, 1997

Dear Elaine and Alex,

We had a wonderful rain last night. It was very unexpected, as far as Quentin and I were concerned. We have both been sleeping good. When Quentin has a good night's sleep he is so dopey in the morning I can hardly stand him.

I don't think I have told you that a week ago on Sunday night I had to hoist him up off the floor three times. That was a record. He fell only once this past week. The first time he was too close to the bed rail and must have been rambunctious, as he knocked the sides down. The other two times he slid out of bed by sitting on the side. I get very aggravated with him when he does that.

A lot of times when he is so dopey he will sit on the edge of the bed and then not get to the urinal on time. I suppose I should say, "It's all right dear. I don't mind picking up your stinking clothes and having wet spots on the carpet." However, that is not my response.

I had two people tell me last week that I needed to get help. Marg said some people think I look worse than Quentin, and she's been asked if I am sick. She suggested I take advantage of the day care program they have at the Cedar's. I won't say the time won't come when I have to do something, but I'm not there yet.

She told me a long time ago that I would look better

with ten pounds more weight. She asked me the other day if I was still losing. I got down to 123 once last week, but I piled on the calories and am back up to 124 or 125.

I've decided it isn't the physical work that's so hard. It's the emotional. I firmly believe I can control that – with a little help. I have made the mistake I have criticized other people for. Got to feeling so good I discontinued using the "mood enhancer" Amitpriptyline. I had been feeling real good for a long time and asked the doctor about discontinuing it. He said I should take it for ninety days. When I ran out of pills it was past ninety days, and I was feeling so good that I just didn't get it refilled.

Was not very long until I was terribly tired again. I was having trouble sleeping. When I woke up in the morning I hurt everyplace. Didn't take me very long to call in a prescription and get back on track. I'm feeling much better again.

Quentin asked this morning if this was Wednesday. When I told him it was Tuesday, he was disappointed. His life has been focused on this class reunion and seeing Avis for months now. I hope she is there and in good physical and mental condition. I hope his classmates are cordial and don't ignore him. He is so hard to talk to that I don't think many people will make an extended effort.

As soon as the reunion is over Quentin will start asking me almost every day if this is the week Elaine is coming. He has not been able to get past the reunion in thinking of the future yet.

Lots of love,

Mom

Dear Elaine and Alex,

Quentin was disappointed that his ex-girlfriend was not able to attend the reunion. She had called the chairman and told him about all of her ailments. Turns out some of them are very serious. At one time Quentin had said, "I feel that Avis is going through a traumatic time."

At 78 years of age, it is quite common to have traumatic times in one's life. I still don't have her address, but am going to get it so we can contact her. Everyone was very friendly with Quentin. He laughed a lot. Afterwards when he said he didn't especially enjoy it, I reminded him that he had laughed a lot. He said, "Well, you can't just sit there."

Congratulations to Alex on that huge donation. I feel it was a personal compliment to you, Alex. The fact that most of the money will go for scholarships is good, too. It shows that you have great management skills when a gift like that doesn't have to go to rescue the operating expenses. I marvel at your job!

I'm also eager to hear how things are at work for you,

Elaine. I am impressed with your ability, too! If your life had gone along the way you had envisioned it at one time, this potential would never have been realized. You would probably be really good on a tractor by now, but you would surely have an aching restlessness and longing for something that no amount of cookies or potato chips could ever fill.

I have to go to work now and get the house clean enough for the cleaning woman.

Lots of love,

Mom

September 12, 1997

Dear Family,

This is going to be a generic letter. I want to tell all of you the same thing, and I spend more time at the computer writing a letter than you can imagine.

I feel exhilarated about Quentin! He is taking only one Valerian Root tablet before going to bed, and he is sleeping like a baby. He goes to bed and settles down immediately without jerking and turning and making all the noises that he did before. He has not been stupid in the night, and has been able to get to the urinal or bathroom every night for almost a week. That sure starts the day off on the right foot for me.

He is more like his "real self" every day. I am

enjoying our life together again and I'm feeling more like my "real self". I think I told all of you that I thought Quentin had a mini stroke not too long ago. The doctor said if it happened again there was medication he could give him, so I will call immediately.

Going to the Vita Belt class at the Fitness Center at the hospital has been a help. When we first started there I got a little impatient at the time the leader spent telling jokes. She would ask what we were going to do over the weekend and then ask about it when we came back on Tuesday. I have certainly changed my mind now. Everyone in that class is "mature" and most have some physical problems. Quentin is the most physically handicapped.

A family feeling has developed, and the people are concerned about each other. The physical exercise is not the only therapy the class provides! One day Quentin felt he was strong enough to walk in on his own. They were so excited he had walked from the parking lot.

Love,

Madelyn

November 3, 1997

Dear Elaine and Alex

We were both so glad to hear that you had prepared your resignation, Alex. We don't feel you need to live with all the stress. It staggers my imagination to even think of all the work involved with such a large institution. The work probably wouldn't be so bad if it weren't for the people on your board of directors.

That is one good thing about farming. Lady landlords can become a cross one has to carry – and the weather and the government and bugs are all problems at various times. But one has the *illusion* of being his own boss, at least. I'm sure you two will find something to do that will be enjoyable for both of you.

On the fourth anniversary of Quentin's stroke he was terribly depressed. He was convinced he was going to die that night, and he wanted to. When we went to bed he told me he didn't know what was going to happen in the night, but if I woke up and he was having a problem, he wanted me to try to go back to sleep and leave him alone.

He woke up alive and fairly cheerful the next morning. I never get excited about death premonitions the way my mother did. Dad could make her jump through a hoop when he would cry and say he was dying. I made three trips to Florida one year. She would call me up crying and upset about him. Frankly, it never made much sense to me, as she had kept a nice black dress in the back of her closet to wear to his funeral since 1946 – and maybe before.

One time when I went to Florida Dad started the crying with me and saying he was going to die. I said I thought death was one of the nicest things God had planned for us. I told him it would be terrible to think a person would have to go on forever in a body that was hurting and didn't work right. I still feel that way. He stopped crying while I was there.

Quentin has been crying a lot. I think this is typical of stroke victims. He has never been quite the same since I told him he couldn't drive me to Wichita. Sometimes it takes him two or more hours to get in gear to get his shoes and socks on.

He doesn't get any sympathy from me for the shape he is in. I reminded him the other evening that he could help himself by exercising. He said he would, but I have to get very insistent to get him on the bike. Quentin does enjoy going to the exercise class at the hospital, but I think most of the good is accomplished by getting out and by being around other people. He can't manage about half of the exercises, and the other half he doesn't do right.

Will be eager to hear from you and learn what has happened. For what it is worth, we will be wishing you the best.

Lots of love,

Madelyn

December 19, 1997

Dear Elaine and Alex,

I called my friend Rene the other day and told her I wanted her opinion on something. I felt that every one in the coffee group had acted rather cold on Friday, and on Sunday people who usually brighten up when they speak to me seemed very reserved. On Sunday afternoon and evening I had a little rhyme from my school days running through my mind — *"Nobody likes me, everybody hates me, I'm going to eat worms and die."* My question to Rene was, "Do I have an aura about me that is turning people off?"

Rene thought for a while, and then she came up with an answer that satisfied me. She said she thinks that everyone is busy with Christmas and their own problems. When I went to coffee yesterday morning everyone seemed friendly again.

I do think a person can put up an invisible barrier around herself.

When I look at myself in the mirror I can't decide if I'm just getting older and uglier, or if I look mean. I think if I were a stranger approaching me on the sidewalk, I might keep my distance for fear I would start hollering orders or shouting obscenities. I really can't understand it. I have accepted the circumstances in my life and decided this is what the situation is and could well be for several years. I will try to make it a learning experience and to live in such a way that I will not have any regrets. I should look like a sweet little old lady, but I don't.

I am so eager to hear your reaction to your Christmas present. I've been giving you hints for months, and you still haven't guessed what it is. Only a few days left before you can open it.

Lots of love,

Madelyn

Chapter 5 - 1998

January 7, 1998

Dear Elaine and Alex,

I'm so glad you liked our present. The daughters-in-law haven't said much. They might not think having a plaster cast of our hands sitting around their houses is such a great thing. Had we known we were going to have it done, we might have filed off the chipped fingernails, but the guy was in the grocery store parking lot and he was just there for one afternoon. He had us hold hands and then dip them in the bucket. I think they turned out pretty good. One of these days when we're both gone, you can look at that little statue and remember the hands that raised you.

We're having terribly cold, icy weather, which means it should be good on the weekend you are coming. I have observed that the weather seems to run in patterns. Good weather usually follows bad (if one waits long enough).

I have been getting Quentin audio books, and he is getting closer to being able to insert a tape into the player and getting it turned on right, but it is still a problem. I can hear him inserting and turning the machine on and off. Unless it gets too bad, I let him struggle with it. For a while I would have to go and turn the tape over every time it had played on one side. It was somewhat of a nuisance, so I have worked with him to do it himself.

His mind is certainly not improving – to put it mildly. The other night he was confused about where the bathroom was. That really alarmed me! He is already asking me almost every day if that is the day you are coming. He is always asking about what day of the week it is. He usually asks me early in the morning if we have to go any place. He gets real confused about doctor appointments.

I am still constantly grateful for his good disposition, his sense of humor, and his love and concern for me. The other night he commented that he didn't know what he would do without me. (He would have to go to a nursing home – that is what he would do!) I feel I have a handle on this situation now, and I'm managing it pretty well emotionally.

He says he doesn't have long to live, so he is not going to eat anything he doesn't like (which includes most vegetables). I think that has something to do with his not making an effort to exercise. He can barely walk now.

Larry took him to Hutchinson to go Christmas shopping. They went to Penny's, and Quentin had to walk quite a ways. They had to get him a chair when he got to the jewelry counter. As I told you, the diamond earrings were quite a surprise. Larry tried to talk him into buying smaller ones, but Quentin wanted me to have the big ones. They are so beautiful, but I don't even want to think about what they cost.

I didn't go out today as the top temperature was 24 and it was icy. Hope I can get to town tomorrow to get our prescriptions and to purchase the journal that goes with the book *Simple Abundance*. It costs $12.95, and I was too tight to buy it when I got the book.

I am supposed to list five things I am grateful for each day. I've been a little stumped this evening. Quentin had the tape on real loud, and it was hard to concentrate when I tried earlier. Maybe I can think of some more things this evening. The author said that some days a person might have to write, "I am grateful to be alive" five times.

There is a lot of Unity in her writing, which is interesting to me. I definitely will not tell Deb, as it would make her stop reading the book. She has told me many times I am going to sizzle in hell because of my belief in Unity's teaching.

I had better go and help Quentin get ready for bed. I have to help him put on the pajama pants, as he will have the legs so messed up. He has trouble getting the top on the right way, so I help with that, too. I put the toothpaste on his brush, fill the Hydra Floss with water, turn it on and off for him. I'm still constantly amazed at the large pieces of food he washes out of his mouth after he's brushed his teeth.

We are certainly anticipating your visit. Looking forward to seeing the kids, too. I'm so glad that Annie is making her arrangements to go to school. I think her choice of training to be a vet tech is an excellent one. I would not be too excited about her wanting to be a vet, as that takes many years of hard work. I don't know whether she would stick to it for all the years it takes.

Well, we should have time to have a good visit when you are here. I have put on my "gratitude list" that I am grateful you and Alex are coming, and I am anticipating being able to say that I am grateful for the wonderful weather we had while you were here.

Lots of love,

Madelyn

February 2, 1998

Dear Elaine and Alex

Quentin has felt terrible all day – still does. He strained and strained to have a bowel movement this morning. I finally had to don the rubber gloves I use for such an occasion and get things going. I hate that job – just about lost my breakfast, but I got through it. He slept for over an hour this afternoon and doesn't feel like listening to a tape or even watching or listening to the Club Dance on the Nashville station. Have tried to get him to go back to bed, but he won't do that. He will probably be all right tomorrow. At least I hope so!

I have come to the conclusion that I have some

unpleasant mental attributes. One is that when I have to do something I don't want to do, I have a terrible physical reaction. Have also discovered when I finally push myself and get the job done that I feel great. I am wondering about my constant running nose. Nothing seems to stop it. I read someplace a long time ago that such a situation was the body weeping. It is an interesting theory at least.

One of the women at the Y commented yesterday that I looked good but had lost a lot of weight. I gave her my usual answer. It is a snap – cut down on sweets and fats and have a semi-invalid husband. There is nothing to it. If Quentin dies before I wear out my size 8 clothes, I will probably have trouble maintaining that size.

Tuesday, February 3

This has been a morning when my neurosis is in full operation. I was reluctant to get up and start a new day. After getting breakfast, doing the dishes and washing a load of clothes, I went back to bed for an hour. After a little consultation with myself and a mental kick in the rear, I finally did get up.

Had planned on going to Hutchinson this afternoon and was going to try to see Annie. I'm so excited about her liking school and doing well. I get a vicarious thrill out of any family member going to college. Will probably call you before you get this letter.

Lots of love,

Mom

February 16, 1998

Dear Elaine and Alex,

I am so happy about your dad that I could shout it from the rooftops. When we went into the Y this morning he didn't want me to get the scooter out. He walked real well with his walker this morning. He did say he was about exhausted by the time he got to the dressing room. But we were in the pool for a good forty-five minutes. It didn't take him long to get dressed today, and he was able to walk out to the car.

I think I told you about Quentin's recent obsession with sex. Last week he asked me if I thought I would ever want to have sex with him again. (We had our last romantic encounter the Sunday before he had his stroke.) I told him that part of our marriage was over. He then asked me if I would mind if he had sex with someone else. I told him it was fine with me. I think I said, "Knock yourself out!"

I thought to myself if he could find someone who wanted to have sex with him, she could have all of him. She could change his soaked sheets in the middle of the night, pick his wet Depends up off the floor, dig the poop out of his rectum when he gets constipated, drag him up off the floor when he falls, etc, etc, etc.

A few days later he said he'd been thinking about Avis, the girl he took to his senior prom. He said he has worried about her and has wanted to contact her. Then he

171

said, "Maybe I shouldn't start something."

He asked if I would to take him to Wichita so he could see her. I finally got her on the phone the other day and told her that Quentin wanted to talk to her. He said she was quite reserved. He has mentioned several times that she sounded so old. She had been to five funerals within the last two weeks and was coming to McPherson for another one on Saturday. She said she would call him sometime when she was in McPherson, as she and her husband both have relatives here.

He asked if it bothered me that he had called her. I told him absolutely not. She has arthritis so bad it is hard for her to get around, and I'm very necessary for Quentin. I don't think either Quentin or Avis would be interested in messing up their marriages. I told him I had not thought there had been a big romance between them when they were in high school. He said they had about four dates. He seems to be over the obsession.

Quentin just shut off *Riders of the Purple Sage* and he will be wanting to go to bed in a few minutes. I'm real tired but want to read for a little bit. I hear the tape going again. We leave the CD player on the dining room table, and he still has a terrible time operating the cassette tapes.

He wants to hear all of my telephone conversations, so he has to shut the tape off when I'm going to use the phone. He pushes almost every button, except the right one. It really doesn't seem that difficult.

I usually let him work with it thinking he will never learn if I do it for him. Sometimes I will hear him turning the tape over and over and then I go out and help him. He has done quite well today. Think he put it on rewind only once.

Love,

Mom

March 18, 1998

Dear Elaine and Alex,

I am so glad that I finally remembered the "Talking Books" program for blind and disabled persons. It is wonderful! The tapes are on four tracks and are definitely long playing. I think it takes an hour to play one side. I talked to the librarian the other day and told her I would like the *Georgia Trilogy* by Eugenia Price. The next day the three books were here.

At first Quentin didn't think he was impressed with Eugenia Price, but he got so interested that he didn't even want to shut it off when we were eating. That sure beats having him sit in the chair with his head down and chin on his chest. That drives me crazy!

As soon as I send one book back, they will send another. It is so easy to close the plastic container the tape comes in. I put the mailing label on the front and stick it in the mailbox. A person is allowed to have as many as ten tapes at a time.

I have been through several days of really miserable depression. Just out of the blue I woke up one morning feeling depressed. I think it started with that book *Simple Abundance*. She said a person should get an artist's sketchbook and fill it with pictures of the home you would like to have; go to a travel agency and get brochures of trips you would like to take, etc., etc.

The author has children in grade school, and I think the book applies to women that age – definitely younger than I am. These things are supposed to help you find your *authentic self*.

I got to thinking back to when I was that age. We were too poor to quit farming. In order to keep our Grade A Dairy status, we were required to build the new milk barn. I learned to milk, and I hated every minute I spent doing it. I also drove wheat trucks that were in terrible condition. I was driving a wheat truck when I was five months pregnant with you!

Trucks didn't have lifts at that time – or at least ours didn't. I would always get out when a truck was lifted with a hoist – just in case it would snap. Didn't think my baby would appreciate that kind of a drop. This was at the time when the women's liberation movement was starting. I would read stories about men becoming impotent because they were having to dry dishes. As I was scooping cow shit out of the barn and sometimes spitting it out of my mouth, I really did not feel very sympathetic toward them. My thoughts were something like, "You poor bastards, my heart aches for you."

As I thought about it, I came to the conclusion that I was being my *authentic self*. I was taking care of my family and helping my husband hold onto what was precious to him. In those days, I don't think we had even heard the word "bankruptcy," and would not have ever considered it. We tightened our belt and worked our way out of it.

It is the same way now – this is not the life either one of us would have chosen, but this is the way it is. I feel that my *authentic self* is fully operational.

During those bad years I often thought it would be convenient if Quentin started drinking or chasing women, then I could have left; but he was always cheerful, hopeful and pleasant. He is still pleasant, but not real cheerful or hopeful any more. He still has a sense of humor and I feel very, very fortunate and appreciative – for both the past years and the present.

During the days of depression I hated my whole routine and had trouble getting anything done. I only wanted to read or sleep. I found Quentin's unpleasant habits very disgusting. Didn't help any when he rolled out of bed two mornings in a row at 3:30 and couldn't get to the bathroom in time.

I turned the mattress, put the side rails on and told him if I caught him sitting on the side of the bed I was going to take a belt to him. I was feeling sorry for myself and I deserved it. Finally, last night I decided I had neglected the true source of help. As I was doing exercises, the Bible verse, "All who are weary and heavy burdened come unto me and I will give you rest," came to me. That was as far as I could get, but that kept going through my head. This morning, I awoke feeling like myself again.

The snow finally quit and the roads are open. Larry has opened our driveway, so we are going to town this afternoon. It is a little after 2:00, and I told Quentin I would be ready to go to town at 3:00. He will hold me to that.

Lots of love,

Madelyn

March 25, 1998

Dear Elaine and Alex,

We have hopes now that spring is coming. We've had sunshine and wonderful temperatures for two days! We didn't get to the Y for two weeks because of the weather, but started again this week, and it was good to be back. Quentin said his digestive system is working better, and he feels very strongly that he is improving.

There is one situation that is bothering me. The plant

you gave us still has blossoms, and Quentin watches it closely. At noon he informed me there were two men by the plant. When I told him I didn't see them he was surprised. I asked what they were doing. He didn't have an answer for that. He said they were little men. When we came home this afternoon and were having our Pepsi, he told me that the men were still there. He has been completely normal about everything else.

He can dress himself pretty well except at night when he is real tired.

He had the top to his pajamas almost on, and I saw it was backward. He didn't want me to change it, but I did. When he was ready to go to bed, he pointed to the bedroom and said, "It is that way, isn't it?"

As we were going to the bedroom he told me he thought he was losing his mind. I didn't agree with him or tell him I was afraid of it too. I told him that was the reason we needed to be exercising – so he would get blood to his brain. He dropped it then.

We are both looking forward so very much to your coming.

Lots of love,
Mom

April 3, 1998

Dear Elaine and Alex,

I called the doctor's office and made an appointment for April 13. I told the woman that Quentin's mental condition was deteriorating, and I had no idea whether it was due to a mini stroke(s) or because of age and physical condition. The doctor was booked up for this week and next. However, she said to call if he got worse and she would see what could be done.

The other night he sweat (it couldn't be classified as perspiring). The water rolled off of him. He wears knit pajamas and he couldn't get the top off because it was sticking to his body so bad. It was a struggle for me to get it off. His first reaction was, "So what?"

He said he would welcome a fatal heart attack. I asked if he'd be open to angioplasty or some of the newer treatments. His comment was that if I wanted surgery I could go have it done to myself.

I have had a lot of observations and thoughts that I would like to share with someone. That is one reason I always enjoy your visits, Elaine. I can share thoughts with you. It is disappointing to realize how few people are interested in such things.

I remember when you first moved away to go to school in Hutchinson how I always anticipated your weekends at home. When you were putting on your makeup I would sit on the toilet stool and tell you what I had read in Unity. I would follow you around every place in the house while you got dressed and ready to go to town. Most people don't have anything to talk about except other people.

We have only been to the Y once this week because of the rain. Hope spring will soon be more than a calendar event. We are enjoying the jonquils that are blooming. The little tree you gave me is fully leafed out. The wheat is such a beautiful green. It is good for the soul after months of seeing all the dull, apparently lifeless ground and trees.

It is Saturday, and as every day, I have a lot to do to try to establish order, so had better get busy. Maybe we can talk on the phone later.

Lots of love,

Madelyn

April 21, 1998

Dear Elaine and Alex,

I've been thinking about Robert all morning. I can't believe he's twenty-one today! I hope if they have a party and do a lot of drinking that they'll have the good sense to not drive. He's such a nice young man. I saw him at Target the other day. He said he's excited to see you. I have really been wheeling and dealing getting ready for your visit. Have gone through all the boxes and piles of junk around the computer and have either thrown away or filed most of my papers. It sure looks and feels better.

Last Saturday, Quentin saw Roland Johnson coming down the road south of us with the road maintainer. I hurried out to the road and stopped him and reminded him that I wanted that trash pit closed. This time I specified before May 1. He came Sunday afternoon and covered it up. It is such a relief to not have to look at it any more. I have hated it for years. Decided I have enough stress, and that there are some things I can eliminate, so I'm in the process of doing that. Right now the man is here cleaning the carpet. My next big job is the sewing room.

I want to get my cupboards cleaned too before you get here. I think you are going to be very tired. What a time you've gone through wrapping up your jobs, selling the house, putting everything in storage and packing for your sixty-day train trip. You will need a chance to decompress to start your vacation. Planting my flowers will help you do that, and of course, you'll have fun with your kids.

I'm looking forward to having you folks so much that it is almost fun doing the work. I'm not doing anything that hasn't needed to be done for a long time. It will make life so much more pleasant and less stressful for me when the jobs are taken care of.

Speaking of jobs – I need for you folks to talk to

Quentin when you're home. He's got it in his head that we could have sex again if "I would just help him." I told him a few weeks ago that wasn't going to happen. The next day he asked me to call Avis. I didn't. He asked the next day, and the next and the next. Finally, it was all he could talk about, so I called her. Avis and her husband drove to McPherson for lunch. (I didn't tell them why Quentin wanted to see her.)

We met at the restaurant. She came in with her oxygen bottle strapped to her walker. She was very frail, and her husband was helping her. He is obviously her caretaker. We had a nice visit, and I thought after seeing her physical condition that Quentin would let it go. But when we got in the car to drive back to the farm, I said, "Well, what do you think about Avis now?" And he said, "I think she wants me!"

I didn't know whether to laugh or cry. I just shook my head and said we needed to hurry back to the farm before he wet his pants. He's been obsessing about her ever since. He says the reason he isn't getting any sex is because I've cut him off, and he keeps badgering me to help arrange things so he and Avis can get together.

All the daughters-in-law are disgusted with him, and none of the boys want to talk to him about it. I hate to ask, but I'd appreciate it if you would be thinking about what you could do to get him to stop talking about it all the time.

On a brighter note – I think it's just wonderful that Alex accepted the job at Oregon State University. I was telling my Friday Morning Coffee Group that he will be teaching a doctoral course in Community College Administration. No one had ever heard of that type of program, but they all thought it sounded interesting.

Quentin is very happy that you two are changing your lifestyle. He has said many times that he was afraid you were pushing Alex too hard. I told him Alex was a college president before you met him and you weren't the one who had pushed him into being a hard worker. He just wants you to have fun and enjoy your lives and each other as long as you can. That's my wish, too.

Well, I must go. We are so happy that everything has worked out so beautifully for you.

Lots of love,

Mom

May 25, 1998

Dear Elaine and Alex,

William Allen White once stated that when he was floating on a pink cloud in heaven, he would think it was just like a June Day in Kansas. Today was a memorable "pink cloud" day. Everything is so beautiful. The weather got up to 76 and the wind didn't blow.

All the flowers you planted are doing fine. The snap

182

dragons are starting to bloom and they have such a variety of colors. I never even knew what dahlias were, and they are doing especially well. They sure are pretty. I'm enjoying all of them.

I am so happy about my new water faucet, Alex, and I'm so glad you suggested it. Years ago when I told Quentin I wanted a faucet on the south side of the house he said I couldn't have one because it would freeze in the winter. When you said, "Why doesn't the faucet on the west side of the house freeze?" I realized I'd been duped! It turned out to be a very expensive pleasure, but it makes the work so much easier. I had been dragging over 100 feet of hose. No wonder I got so skinny!

That faucet comes under one of the nice things I have done for myself, which would be approved of by the woman who wrote *Simple Abundance*. I haven't gotten into baths by candlelight, and I don't have a drawer with goodies for bad days – I guess I'm still on the practical side.

We've had quite a time about Avis since your visit. A week ago Saturday afternoon I was in the living room and heard Quentin bellering. He does that when he hits a sad spot in a book. I couldn't think what could have been that sad in the book he was listening to. The crying continued and got louder, so I decided he wanted me to hear him. I went in the dining room and asked if he had hit a sad spot. He said, "No, I'm just afraid that I have hurt you. Elaine really scolded me about Avis."

I guess he's been thinking about your conversation. He sure hadn't considered the practical side of things before that, including the physical conditions of everyone involved. Have to admit I thought it was pretty funny when you said, "Dad, think about the logistics! Mom would have to drive you to a hotel, and Avis' husband would have to drive her. Then what the hell would they do while you and Avis are in the room having sex?"

At any rate, I had hoped that would be the end of it, but he still had sex on the brain, so I decided it was time to have the talk you suggested. I proceeded to tell him how lucky he'd been to be able to have sex so long, and I reminded him about all of the men we've known who became impotent much earlier than he did. I repeated the story that I had been told about an old woman who married an old man. According to her friend "He rode her all night for four nights. On the fifth night she went to a separate bedroom, locked the door and started divorce proceedings the next day."

He sat there looking petulant. When I finished that story he said, "Yes, but he married again before long and didn't have any trouble."

I reminded him that this incident happened to a couple in Indiana and that we had no idea if he got married again afterward. He said that I should hit him in the head and be done with it. My reply was, "Don't tempt me."

Anyhow, last Wednesday evening he decided that the situation around here was back to a normal state of confusion, so he wanted to go see Avis. I called her. I'd told her some time back why he'd been wanting to get together with her.

When we were talking on the phone I told her Quentin still wanted to see her. She laughed in such a way that I could tell she was enjoying the situation. Anyhow, she called Saturday morning to tell me they were coming to McPherson. They came out to the farm and we were able to show them the hoist, which had been one thing important to Quentin. We went to lunch at the Chinese restaurant. Avis and I like each other, and we talked a mile a minute.

Afterwards, Quentin said he was glad he didn't marry her – she laughed too much. He still wants a chance to visit with her. He said the only time he got to talk to her was when I was in the bathroom. I think we will go to Wichita and I will have my friend Vera meet us. Vera and I will take a table to ourselves and let them talk.

Avis and I had just a short time to visit alone. She told her cousin, who goes to the same beauty shop about Quentin's infatuation. All of the gals at the beauty parlor got a big kick out of it. I told her I had dragged my feet wondering what her husband would think. She admitted that he thought it was strange. His hearing is worse than mine, and he was very reserved at first. By the time they left though, he was urging us to come see them.

Years ago Quentin told me he didn't want to marry her as their kids would have looked like squirrels. She definitely needed braces when she was young. Quentin has always said that of all the things his folks did for him, he appreciated the braces on his teeth the most. He insists Avis has had a face lift and she doesn't look like she used to. I got out her picture and the one of me taken in 1945 and asked if I still looked the same.

The only picture we have of her is the one taken the night of the prom. I reminded Quentin that he didn't look the same as he did at that time, and if she would have seen him on the street or someplace else, she would never have recognized him. After all, it was sixty-one years ago when they went to the prom.

She kissed Quentin on the cheek when she left. I told her that I had told my family I hoped she and Quentin would develop a torrid romance and I would be glad to give him to her. The experience turned out to be very pleasant, and I do look forward to seeing them again.

The sex matter still hasn't been resolved completely. The other evening Quentin said there were several things he wanted to ask the doctor about the next time we went, which will be tomorrow. He was going to ask if he would hurt me if we had sex. I reminded him again that sex was over for him. After all, he had a double whammy with the stroke and the shots for his prostate cancer.

I saw in the paper that Bob Dole is taking Viagra to relieve his impotence. Quentin has heard the ads for Viagra, but it hasn't registered with him. He would probably want to try it. I feel detached from all this, and it is less troublesome than some other things. I feel sorry for him and regret the condition of his mind, which is getting worse. Thank goodness he hasn't been disagreeable or mean.

I received your card from Philadelphia. I can't remember the Carter House, but I was probably there. I am vicariously enjoying your trip – have looked up places on the Atlas. I have tried to find Quincy, but have not had any luck. I look forward to hearing your reaction to Niagara Falls. I'm sure it will be like ours. There is no picture that does the experience justice. We were driving to Toronto to a cow show and stopped there. We could hear the roar miles away, and while we weren't in a dangerous position, we could feel the spray. It was in November and cold, but it was a thrill.

The timeshare in Williamsburg sounds wonderful. I would guess you are enjoying being alone with the room to spread out almost as much as you are enjoying the sightseeing. Quentin and I have always enjoyed having "separateness in our togetherness" when we were with other people for a while. I even wanted that in our relationship with each other – more than Quentin did.

We had a doctor appointment this morning. I was shocked when we were told that Quentin's latest PSA test showed 5.1. In December it was 1.6, and before that it had registered at 0.4 or less. I asked what could be done about it and was told there was nothing. The male nurse asked Quentin if he had any new pains or problems. Quentin told him that he couldn't get an erection. The nurse looked at me and shook his head slightly.

I'm feeling so much better emotionally – and you might think this is crazy, but Betty, the cleaning woman, has gotten into Flower Essence. She said she had been burdened with a feeling of not being treated fairly –that feeling and her depression disappeared without any effort on her part except taking four drops of the Flower Essence that deals with those problems.

She gave me a list of the different flowers. A person can order for six different problems and they will be blended. All of the ones she ordered for me had to do with feeling burdened. I feel free of that feeling, and it is a great relief. Sounds crazy, but if it works, why knock it?

As I have said before, I am thoroughly enjoying your trip and have fun visualizing the various places you have been and have yet to go.

Lots of love,

Madelyn

June 8, 1998

Dear Elaine and Alex

As you know by now, I asked Keith and Vivian to deliver this letter to you. Do you think I'm being cheap or efficient? We received your card and letter today with the information on all the places you're visiting. I looked through everything and enjoyed it, but haven't studied it in detail. I just know I would like to be there with you. I'm so grateful for the time you and I shared in New York five years ago, Elaine. I wouldn't take any amount of money for that time.

Enjoyed the Coffee Group this morning. We were on a high level. One woman wanted to know if we knew the difference between the first and second honeymoon — the first one is Niagara, the second one is Viagra.

Norma is of the opinion that someone should send Ken Star a sex manual. She thought maybe that would end his curiosity. On the noon news yesterday there was a story about a couple getting married. She was 82 and he was 91. They both said that intimacy was important. They went on to tell that a lot of nursing homes prohibited "intimacy" between residents. This couple thought what they did in privacy was their own business. Norma didn't think there could be much privacy since the doors in most nursing homes don't have locks. Guess they'll have to find a "Do Not Disturb" sign like a person can get in a motel room.

I told the women about this couple and you should have heard the negative comments. They were all of the opinion that "intimacy" at that age was ridiculous, and none of them were interested. I didn't tell them that I had threatened to put Quentin in the nursing home in Inman where one of the old ladies goes from room to room trying to get into bed with the male residents.

Quentin is doing much better. He is determined we are going to go to Wichita next week to see Avis. I told him I would call Vera. She could come meet us, and she and I would have our lunch together so he and Avis could visit, but Quentin doesn't want me to leave. He would probably like for Avis and I to not spend so much of the time talking. He seems to have the sex situation in the proper perspective. Last week was wonderful. He was a lot like himself and I enjoyed him. This week is starting out good.

Ran into a friend in town who said her kids wanted her to get a computer. She said she didn't need one. She can click on her memory file and bring up anything she wants to. I told her that I did have a computer, but I also had an extensive memory file. My memory file comes in color and has fragrances and emotions. It is not a black and white account of facts. I told her (and it is the truth) that sometimes I have to feel my toothbrush to see if I have brushed my teeth, but I haven't lost my long-term memory files.

I'm enjoying the new water faucet so much. I might get to like this pampering myself. Still haven't been able to buy any chocolate truffles to put in my dresser drawer, but who knows, I might get there someday!

Quentin is ready for bed, so I had better go. I am enjoying your trip and my mental movie has been very busy recording you every day. That is the advantage of having a mental movie that goes full time when reading or visiting with people. I can anticipate the fun you will have with Keith and Vivian in Canada. I thought of something the other day I wish you had included in your trip. I wish you could have gone to the Paradise Inn on Mt. Rainier. You have a short time between trains in Seattle, but it is not enough to take that trip. The memories of the two days we spent there on our honeymoon got us through the 32 months Quentin was overseas during World War II.

Lots of love,

Madelyn

June 28, 1998

Dear Elaine and Alex,

I am getting new digital hearing aids this week. They had an enticement. They would give a person full purchase price for the present ones. It still cost me an additional $2,400. I wrote to our banker and told him I needed a somewhat impartial person to give me advice. I told him how Quentin often says, "Do you have the damn hearing aids in?" I also told him that Quentin had always wanted me to have the best, so he would not be impartial. I told him my goal was to get the line of credit completely down, and I was uncomfortable spending the money on myself.

The banker called back and said that the crops weren't as good as last year and the price wasn't as good either; however, he told me to get the digital hearing aids. He also shocked me when he said that Greg had talked to him three or four times and told him if we ever needed help, to be sure to let him know. He and Deb have been so generous.

After Quentin and I had our talk about sex, which you recommended, he seems to have accepted the situation. He now acts as if it had never been part of his life, and he doesn't show any outward signs of bitterness about it. He still wants to go to Wichita to see Avis, but that is under control now, too. I had written to Greg and Deb and told them about the Avis situation, which I thought was more amusing than anything. They seemed real disgusted.

I have written them a letter tonight telling them I was sorry they felt the way they did about Quentin. I think my insight was right about him feeling like he had lost control of everything else and his body was his last stand.

I told you about the Flower Essence, and it has really

helped (I think). Maybe being more accepting has helped, too. I have always been good to Quentin, but I have a different attitude now, and he has responded very well. We have enjoyed a very pleasant relationship and companionship the last two or three weeks. I think we are probably in for a long haul, and I would not be surprised if this continues for another five years. Frankly, I do not anticipate celebrating our sixtieth wedding anniversary. We will celebrate our fifty-sixth this September.

I think the greatest expression of love is to release a person. I have wondered if funeral homes give out printed instructions on how women should respond to their husband's death. It seems that it doesn't matter how unhappy a marriage had been, the correct response is, "I don't know how I will live without him," or "I miss just having him around." What crap!

I have been told a number of times how lucky I am to have Quentin still alive. Some of the standard comments gag me. Even when I was very young, I used to say that if I had an unhappy marriage, when he died I would say, "I'm glad you are gone, you old bastard!"

Lots of love,

Madelyn

July 23, 1998

Dear Elaine and Alex,

I'm thrilled about your new house. The location is as much an asset as the house itself – I would guess. I have such a thing about trees that it would please me very much.

I'm getting involved in something new that is very exciting to me. Alex may have heard of Reiki when he was in Japan. The word means Universal Life. Reiki is a method of healing by touch. I'm going to take a course. It will cost $100, but will include three Reiki sessions. I'm enclosing the booklet that I got last night.

I can visualize Quentin having pain before he gets out of this world, and I would like to be able to help him. Reiki does not interfere with medicine or any other treatments. With a background of Unity and Reflexology, and the desire to help people, I do not expect any trouble in learning or accepting this.

For the most part things are going pretty good with Quentin. He has been very accepting of my studying Reiki. He is starting to talk about how we have to go to Wichita to see Avis again. He keeps saying she will be worried about us. I told him I would get her on the phone tonight and she could talk to him.

If I don't get to town I will miss the mail again today. Will probably talk to you on the phone before you get this. I have re-read that little pamphlet several times and wonder if you will think Reiki is rather kinky. It isn't really. Will look forward to telling you more about it.

Lots of love,

Madelyn

July 29, 1998

Dear Elaine and Alex,

On Saturday morning Quentin told me it was very painful for him to urinate. I hurriedly called the doctor – couldn't get ours, so I talked to the one on call. He called in a prescription. Quentin has been incontinent for two days now. He was better on Saturday, but he was a mess yesterday. I have had him in Depends. Yesterday he wouldn't even try to go to the bathroom. When I went to the dining room to fix our supper, there was a puddle under his chair. That makes me lose my good disposition.

I went to see Rose Morris, my Reiki instructor Saturday afternoon, and we had a wonderful time together. When I went to the meeting Wednesday night I was amazed at how many Unity terms were used – such as Mind, Soul and Body, Transition, I Am. Through Reiki a person is a channel for the Universal Life Force, which we all have.

After the first meeting I picked up a Unity book by Emmett Fox entitled, *The Sermon on the Mount*. I was very surprised to find the words "Universal Life Force" right away. Later I got out my book on Chinese Internal Exercises. They use the word "Chi" to explain the Universal Life Force. They stress that it is not the individual doing the healing. It is God.

I had told Jean a little bit about it, and when she called yesterday she wanted to know how I got along with my voodoo class. It is far from that.

Thursday, July 30

I will eventually get this letter written. Quentin has been wanting to talk to Avis, so we finally got her on the phone tonight. She was telling me about getting the heel of her shoe stuck in some tar as they were leaving a restaurant. In trying to get out, she got the other shoe stuck. Her husband is almost stone deaf, so he didn't hear her calling, and finally looked to see where she was. He came to pull her out, and someone going past offered to help, but she didn't want a stranger pulling on her. She hurt her neck in the process. Quentin surprised me with his very common sense solution. He said, "Why didn't she just walk out of her shoes?"

It seemed so absolutely simple. That is the common sense kind of solutions he always used to have. Every so often he comes up with something like that and it almost makes me cry.

Love,

Mom

August 9, 1998

Dear Elaine & Alex,

Quentin is doing better but still isn't completely over his trouble. We had quite a discussion about his not doing anything to help himself. He has told me he will soon be 80, so he can't see any reason to try to prolong life. I told him I was going to take him to the Cedars and let him ride down the hall and see the condition of the residents in there. People can live for years in a helpless, barely alive state, long after their time clock should have run out. I told him I was not going to ruin my back or guts helping him if he won't help himself. That doesn't seem to motivate him, though.

We called Avis the other evening. She and her husband purchased a home in a retirement community in Augusta. She said she wanted us to come down and see the home where they have lived for the last 45 years. This evening Quentin told me that Avis wanted him to kiss her when she was here – which I seriously doubt. I told him he'd better not try it, as her husband could well object.

Monday

Teri and Larry are having bank trouble again. Larry has said many times he wouldn't go through what he did the last time, and that he would just let the bank have every-thing. He's changed his attitude now and is determined to make a go of this. In the last five years he has had two new pickups, and they've bought three new cars. They had a minivan that was much newer than ours, but Teri wanted a regular van so she would have room for all the grand-babies. Larry said they might not have the money next year for a new car, so they decided to buy it while they could.

I understand Reiki brings up memories and angers that need to be addressed. The other evening I told Quentin he was never interested in listening to me until after he had his stroke. When I used to try to share or read things of a spiritual nature to him he would be nice and listen, but it was easy to tell that he was glad when he could get away from me. He was a little shocked when I told him that.

I reminded him he has only been interested in learning since the stroke. He commented one day that I was so far ahead of him. I told him since all he'd ever thought about was the farm that I had developed the spiritual and mental side of me and had my own world. I'm especially grateful for that now. It takes everything I have to be able to cope with this situation. When I think it is almost five years and no end in sight, I'm glad for my own mental and spiritual world.

Seems as if all I have done in this letter is bitch – maybe lots of things are coming up that need to be addressed.

I've been thinking about both of you. This summer has

sure been a good experience in regaining your energy and enthusiasm. I'm glad you both are excited about leaving off your old life and starting a new one. I'm also glad you both appreciate nature so much – that is a spiritual experience in itself. Quentin and I look back on the ten weeks we spent in Florida in 1993 as the best time of our lives. I don't expect we will ever have that kind of experience again, but there are sure good memories that we can relive over and over.

It is almost 10 pm. Quentin seems to be engrossed in a new tape, but he will be calling pretty soon that he is ready to go to bed. Think I will beat him to it tonight.

Lots of love,

Mom

August 21, 1998

Dear Elaine & Alex,

I am now certified to do Reiki. I gave Quentin a treatment last night and he loved it. He said he would like to have that every night – and he will. The heat from the hands feels so good.

The anticipation of the trip to Oregon has spurred Quentin to exercise. He is excited at the thought of celebrating our 56th wedding anniversary at Mt. Rainier. He can see how much he needs to exercise. One time when I was talking about having a wheel chair at the airport, he

199

said he didn't need it. He admits now that he does.

I'm afraid if we wait too long the Paradise Inn will be snowed in. I don't know what the situation with the weather is now, but Quentin remembered that the Inn was going to close the day we left, which would have been around September 9, 1942. There were lots of people there on Labor Day, but I can't remember anyone else being there on Tuesday.

It was in November, before Thanksgiving, that the army took a truck load of men, including your father, to Mt. Rainier to go skiing. They anticipated some of the men might be shipped to the European Theater, and skiing was a skill they might need.

I would guess we might have to wait until spring, but I haven't told Quentin. You wouldn't want him in your lovely new home until he gets this prostate condition taken care of.

Larry sure isn't taking care of himself. He is overweight, smokes, has high blood pressure and is a borderline diabetic. In addition to which, he is a terrible worrier. We pray for him every night that he will accept the guidance available to him in relationship to the management of his money and the care of his body.

I haven't told Deb and Greg about the Reiki. Deb would probably think I was into Satanism or something like that. Unity is bad enough. She doesn't believe anyone can be "saved" or have the Spirit of God unless he has confessed Jesus Christ as his/her savior. Once I quoted the Bible verse, "Know ye not that your body is a holy temple and that God dwells in it?"

The practice of Reiki came from the Japanese, and I doubt she would accept that they know anything about the Universal Life Force or the healing power within each person. Will mention it to her when I see her, but don't think it wise to try to write about it in a letter.

Hope all is going well with you folks.

Love you both,

Mom

September 1, 1998

Dear Elaine and Alex,

Quentin and I just came in from walking. He does much better in the morning than at night. He got along fine riding his bicycle this afternoon for two miles. We went to the pool on Monday and plan on going again tomorrow. He sure wants to go to Oregon. I personally feel it might be better if we waited until spring, but I'm not going to make that suggestion to him. Who knows what could happen to him this winter. He hasn't had any trouble with the prostate for a couple days now, so hopefully it might be under control.

I have been giving Quentin a Reiki treatment every night when he goes to bed and he sure is sleeping better.

I don't think I get out of the room before he is asleep. I have been working on his right hand and was pleased yesterday to see him using it a lot more than he usually does. I commented on it last night and said I was pleased. I haven't seen him use it at all today.

Have been having a lot of trouble with my legs at night and I've treated them. I think my trouble is that I can't keep my mind clear. A lot of unimportant thoughts keep going through my mind. Will feel I've accomplished something if I ever get to the place where I can "go into the silence." The practitioners always acknowledge that it is God's healing force that takes place. Reiki is not a religion. It is a treatment.

Quentin said last night he's sure he can make the trip. He told me to find out how soon Mt. Rainier will be snowed in. The medicine he's taking seems to be doing the trick for him. Don't think he's been wet all day, and that is a relief for both of us.

He is listening to an interesting book right now. It is the story of the events leading up to World War II and the effect it had on one family's life. He's enjoying it, even though it does bring back a lot of very vivid memories.

I am so excited about the fiction writing course you are taking, Elaine. I took an English Comp class several years ago, and I enjoyed it so much. I was always so excited I couldn't go to sleep for a long time on the night of the class. Will be vicariously enjoying your classes with you.

Lots of love,

Mom

September 17, 1998

Dear Elaine and Alex,

I wrote several pages to you the other night, but it was all bitching, and I decided I didn't want to send it. I was so angry with myself Sunday morning. I didn't even ask Quentin if he wanted to go to church. I knew there were going to be a lot of people there – former members and ministers. As I was getting ready to go, I looked out the bathroom window and saw Quentin sitting in a chair in front of the garden. He was in the sun. I went out and asked if he would like to be moved to the shade. He said the sun felt good on his shoulders, so I let it go. As I was leaving he was all slumped over in the chair in his frequent position. I waved, and he waved back rather half-heartedly.

After I got to church I was thinking that I could have gotten some of the big guys to help get him upstairs, and I was feeling guilty. Dr. Sherry read a poem that was written by a woman in a nursing home a few days before she died. It was not found until they were cleaning out her things. She started out by stating how she seemed to

After I got to church I was thinking that I could have gotten some of the big guys to help get him upstairs, and I was feeling guilty. Dr. Sherry read a poem that was written by a woman in a nursing home a few days before she died. It was not found until they were cleaning out her things. She started out by stating how she seemed to appear to them – a grouchy old woman. Then she recalled the years starting when she was 18 and eager to get married. By the time she was 25 she had her family. She continued to go through the various stages and then said, "Why don't you ever see me? All you see is a grouchy old woman."

I didn't get quite all of it, but she was telling how people treated her. I was sitting by a couple from Ellinwood. He cried so hard (without making a sound) that the bench shook. It was our 56th wedding anniversary. I was thinking about going back to the Paradise Inn on Mt. Rainier. I got started crying and could not stop. When I went to the basement for coffee and cake I was barely under control. Charles Prather was standing by the serving table. I told him to not sing Happy Anniversary or I would start crying again. He said he had already been told by two people to do it. He didn't, however.

When I came home I told Quentin about it and I cried some more. He said he felt like crying, too, but didn't. I must confess there are times when I see a rather repulsive old man rather than really seeing Quentin. Later he told me that he often feels like a nobody. When he is in a group and conversation is being bounced around he wants to participate, but by the time he forms in his mind what he wants to say the conversation has moved on. I have been making a special effort to sit in a chair in the dining room and talk to him – or to ask what was on the news if he has been watching that.

He is looking forward to this trip so much – and to going to Mt. Rainier. He said one night that he wanted to take this trip, then he wants to have his 80th birthday and after that he would be ready to go. My comment was that he probably wouldn't be so lucky.

I forgot to tell you that we had lunch with Avis and her husband on Tuesday. We met them at the Amarillo Bar and Grill and then went to their house. As we were coming home Quentin said that would be the last time we saw them. He said he was over her. He said he lost his nerve to ask her if she had a face lift or had something done to her jaw. He doesn't think she looks anything like she did sixty years ago. I told him again that he doesn't look the same either. I think she has changed very little during the years.

We are anticipating seeing your house and all the wonderful things you have to show us. It won't be long now!

I went to coffee this morning – told them the joke about Hillary Clinton changing her name to Sharon Peters. Even the radical Democrats in the group got a kick out of that. Most of us are Republicans, but we respect the right to disagree. We have to be very careful about what we say.

I received your beautiful birthday card today and the airline tickets. Thank you very much. I bought a new purse yesterday, which is quite large. I'm trying to get used to it. This will eliminate a carry-on bag. I have put the tickets in it. If I were to put them in a safe place somewhere in the house where I would remember them – I probably would never be able to find them again.

Lots of love,

Madelyn

P.S. Leave Wichita 8:10 am, Arrive Portland 1:49 pm

Photo Oposite Page

September 1998 – Quentin & Madelyn's 56th Anniversary at Mount Rainier, Washington.

October 20, 1998

Dear Elaine and Alex,

It has been almost three weeks since we came home from Oregon, and I haven't written you a thank you letter. We do thank you. I have wonderful memories, and I am so glad we were able to be there. The movie in my  mind has been going full blast. When I need a quick vacation I can close my eyes and see the beautiful sights on Mt. Rainier. Sometimes I go to the ocean.

Right now I am visualizing you Elaine, in your office working on your story for this week. Sometimes my movie is working at your home. Sometimes people will say, "It's too bad your trip was spoiled by Quentin's health problems." We only lost two-and-a-half days, but there were still a lot of good days left.

It hasn't been an interesting or fun time since we've been home. The operation will take care of Quentin's immediate prostate problem, but it is taking time to get back to a normal schedule for him. So far he has been able to use the urinal only once. By the time he realizes he needs to go to the bathroom it's too late to get there. When I was stripping and changing his bed last night I couldn't help but comment that there sure were advantages to the catheter.

I enjoyed having Gloria here. As I told everyone, I could have gotten Quentin checked in without help. I've done it so many times, but Gloria is very thoughtful and it was a help. She said I needed to go to a therapist to overcome, as she perceives it, my problem with not being interested in sex. I think if she lived with Quentin for a while she could understand why I have said, "I am through."

She thought it was shocking when I said I would not remarry. She couldn't see why I wouldn't be willing to get married if some handsome, interesting man were to come along after I became a widow. That conversation certainly points out the changes that take place with age and conditions. She was very indignant about Avis and couldn't understand why I wasn't upset about it.

I have certainly been reminded of the situation with my dad. I used to tell Mother that he was not operating with a full deck and she had to take that into consideration. That is the way Quentin is. You mentioned, Elaine, that his mind is as sharp as a tack. He is sharp about things in the past. He certainly isn't about the present. There is one thing that most people cannot see – basically, he has not changed. Years ago lots of people would say that no one but me could live with Quentin. I never understood what they were talking about, and I still don't understand why they said that.

I have never tried to put anyone in a box of my own making. When Mother was here before Greg was born she was telling me things about Quentin that I should change. I finally told her that I wasn't perfect, and until I was, I couldn't expect him to be. I did tell her though, that when I became perfect he had better watch out! He has not been in danger of having to become perfect during the intervening years.

I think I learned at the first cow show we attended that on show day, I was not his number one priority. I stayed as far away from him as possible. I had fun visiting with the other women or going into the town or doing something else interesting. I didn't sit around sulking and feeling sorry for myself. It was the same way with the farm. He was always busy, and we had no social life in the usual sense. I built my own life. When he told me he was retiring I told him that I had built a life of my own and I was not going to give everything up so I could baby-sit with him. I have gone so many places alone that I have said several times if I had any sex appeal I would have been asked for a date.

October 24,

My letter writing got side-tracked someplace during the last few days. I have Quentin in bed tonight, so I will see what I can do. He started passing blood in his urine yesterday. This evening he was so discouraged because he couldn't urinate. He finally did, and he passed a blood clot about three inches long. I called the hospital and was told it was normal after that surgery, but if he got weak or dizzy from the lack of blood that I should take him to the hospital.

Greg is coming Wednesday. He would have come for the surgery, but I didn't ask him to. I don't want to become dependent on the family to handle things. It would certainly be an easy thing to do. I appreciated the help you and Alex gave when we were there, and as I said, it would sure be easy to call for help every time. Larry had been rained out, and I was lucky. I had to call him three times the first night we were home to come get Quentin off the floor. He offered to take Quentin to the hospital on Monday to have the catheter taken out, but I told him I could handle it.

Sunday

I'm so glad you're enjoying the computer. Elaine, your fiction writing course sounds wonderful. It sounds better than a creative writing course. I don't think I would be good in either one. I get lots of ideas of things that would make a good story, but I've never gotten anything but letters down on paper.

I get a lot of joy from the way you two enjoy and appreciate your lives. The wisdom and ability to be that way is not appreciated and used by most people. Quentin always said that if he could be anywhere and do anything in the world he wanted to, he would be right here doing exactly what he was doing. I felt like he was a millionaire, as most people cannot make that statement. I certainly can't.

I must go! Love you both!

Madelyn

November 5, 1998

Dear Elaine and Alex,

I remember 20 years ago today when Annie was born. My mother was on the third floor of the hospital, my dad was on first in Geriatrics and you were on second. I was so thrilled for you to have a daughter!

We got the copy of your short story today and we enjoyed it very much. I marveled at your idea. I would think if you wanted to sell it, you might start by seeking a magazine that is written for Hispanic Catholics. In view of the fact that I have never written anything and have never looked for a market, my thoughts might be way off.

Would be interested in your story on conflict. You might have trouble picking a single incident in your life to write about. They tell a person to write what she knows about, so you probably came up with a good story using a combination of events. Thanks for sending the story.

We will enjoy reading anything and everything you write.

I don't think I have told you about the present I got for Quentin for our wedding anniversary. We're both real happy with it. He never told me he wanted anything until the day before our anniversary, and then he said he wanted a wedding band. I went to town on Saturday afternoon and was shocked that there was only one jewelry store open. The cheapest band they had was over $300, and that was out of my price range.

I went into Prairie Gold on Tuesday, and they had one that looked the same for $151, so I bought it. I had it gift-wrapped and proudly gave it to Quentin. The day he was having surgery he didn't want to take it off. The nurse wrapped gauze and tape around it. He had no trouble leaving his billfold in his side table.

I've been thinking a lot about Gloria saying I needed to go to a therapist. I have thought of the different stages of life that come naturally with the aging process. I was so thrilled to be pregnant with Larry – it was like a song in my head, "I'm going to have a baby."

One night I had Quentin's folks, George and Eva and Elizabeth Arnold out for the evening. I felt sorry for those women since they couldn't have babies any more. I even thought they might be envious of me.

When you were a baby I would sit and hold you to feed you. Sometimes it was a challenge with the three boys running loose. I can remember saying that you would only be a baby once and there would still be housework to do when I had grandkids. Smart young woman, wasn't I?

I remember one of Mother's neighbors coming to see her. She was raving about a new polish she had found for cleaning door knobs and cupboard handles. I never asked what it was, as I still haven't polished door knobs or cupboard handles. Once in a while I have swished a wet cloth over them to get the sticky stuff off. I don't know why that incident made me think of a stage of life.

I am at the stage of life now that I am thrilled about finding the "Slip-on Absorbent Undergarment" made by Target and the wonder of those blue plastic pads for the bed. I'm just dying to find someone who would be interested in knowing about them.

I don't think a person would have to be a certified therapist to understand why at this stage of life I'm not interested in sex. I suppose I have linked the doorknob polish to my exciting new "finds". It would probably take someone who has walked in my shoes for the last five years to fully understand.

A couple women in the coffee group commented that I needed to have more in my life than just Quentin. I feel that I do. I try to get to the Friday Morning Coffee, church on Sunday, the Fellowship Group and Meals on

Wheels board meetings. The thing I enjoy the most, though, is the time after I get Quentin to sleep.

After I give him his Reiki treatment, he usually goes to sleep like a baby. If I were to be asked what my favorite avocation is, I would not have any trouble saying reading is first. Writing letters comes next. I feel pretty good if I get to bed by midnight. It is the 1:00 o'clock nights that leave me tired. A lot of times Quentin will start stirring around 1:00. I hurry and get my pajamas on and turn the lights off, so if he wakes up I can say that I got up to go to the bathroom. We "kids" have our little games, don't we?

Lots of love,

Mom

November 18, 1998

Dear Elaine and Alex,

We will be thinking of you on your birthday, Elaine, as we do every day, but this will be special. I will never forget standing at the nursery window at that hospital and watching you try to turn over. You were determined to walk when you were seven months old. Most babies are just learning to crawl at that age.

There was no place I could put you where you didn't end up falling, except maybe the high chair. You would try to walk in your bed, in the playpen, between chairs.

214

You didn't want to waste time getting down on the floor, crawling to the chair and getting up again. You didn't handle heat well. Frankly, about this time I was wondering why I had wanted a girl so bad! There was merit to little boys who were content to sit quietly and take all their toys apart. You learned to walk by the time you were nine months old, and you were a joy again – and have been ever since.

I think after all these years you are finally in a position to stop pushing, and you can finally relax and enjoy life. Alex is a big help in your achieving that ability, and we are grateful for you, Alex.

I know you will have a wonderful time with Jean and Frank and with Alex's family at Disney World. Frank is one of a kind. So is Jean. They are both good people and have many admirable qualities. They are great about visiting sick people and being faithful to friends. They do have a few quirks, though. Jean likes reading the *Enquirer*. She said that most authors are homosexuals, and she doesn't want anything to do with them. Guess you will have to get published so she will know at least one author isn't gay.

Lots of love,

Mom

December 2, 1998

Dear Elaine and Alex,

I'm sorry I upset you with my "down" the other day. I wasn't feeling good, which contributed to it. The pain was probably coming from the arthritis I have in my breast bone. It was so sore the other day, and it was very painful to touch. I massaged it, and the trouble has almost gone away. I think the present circumstances put my imagination to work thinking "what if." Shows a person what the mind can do.

'I started affirming that I was being healed. As a matter of fact, the affirmation is, "Christ in me is restoring me to wholeness and health, and I give thanks." I have read that most sickness starts in the mind. That is encouraging to me, because I know I can control my thinking.

This has been quite a week for deaths: three friends have died. I am now the sole survivor of all the people who worked at Morris and Son during the War. I started there when I was 19.

I am anticipating the coffee at Lucy Johnson's tomorrow morning. Her house will probably be well-decorated. It is amazing how many homes are decorated and lighted. Looks as if there were an unspoken agreement that McPherson would make Christmas beautiful. Makes me think I should go upstairs, bring down my Christmas tree and plug it in.

I have been thinking I would like to have a pet. I asked the group this afternoon if they thought that would be good for Quentin. This morning I said something about it to him, and his immediate reaction was, "Wait until I am gone." I've thought maybe an animal would supply some of the loving Quentin thinks he isn't getting – do you suppose?

I have had an idea for Quentin's birthday, which I will throw out. I've thought about renting the room where you had the graduation party for Robert and Jennifer. We could have a light lunch with sandwiches and potato chips and things like that.

I would invite relatives and special friends. Quentin says all he wants is a card shower, but I think he would like more. I don't want to say anything to him at this stage, as he would be asking me every day if this were the day of the party.

I would like your reaction to this – either good or bad – and suggestions for change. I want to make it as easy as possible. I might even check with Sirloin Stockade to see how much they would charge to serve everything. I know it would be a lot more money, but we might decide it was worth it.

Speaking of Quentin – in some ways he is improving. His bladder control is better. He's been dry all day for several days. This morning he got a pair of shorts out of the drawer and did not want to wear a pad. He has gotten along fine. The doctor assured us that he would eventually get his control back.

Most of the time his mind is fairly good – about like it was when we were in Oregon. Other times it isn't good. He was awake one night and told me there was a big snake in his bed. I helped him get up and into the dining room. I made some hot milk. When we were through I mentioned going back to bed. He told me he was afraid to, as that snake might still be there. Another time I fussed with him for sitting on the edge of the bed. He told me he had put a milk can under the mattress, so sitting on the edge wouldn't hurt it. He was even going to show me the milk can.

I enjoyed the coffee at Lucy Johnson's yesterday morning. Those women do such a beautiful job of serving. Lucy has carpal tunnel syndrome and is very limited in the use of her hands. She said she doesn't have any of the other problems that beset an aging person, and she has just accepted this. I don't think I would be as accepting. My lifestyle needs both hands, a clear mind, a strong back and generally good health. Fortunately, I have not had any shortness of breath or chest pains since last Monday.

I have to run or it will be lunch time. When Quentin sees the hands on the clock at 12:00, he says it is time to eat.

Lots of love,

Mom

December 10, 1998

Dear Elaine & Alex,

Since I can't discuss the birthday celebration on the telephone, I will write and tell you my plans. When Greg was here I asked him to take me to Perkins. The woman in charge of parties was wonderful to work with. She gave me a menu and suggested the roast beef, which she said people like real well. She said it has no fat. There are vegetables served on top, a potato, rolls and salad – plus coffee or tea. The cost will be $10.20 per person, which includes the gratuity. She said we could bring our own cake.

It is a great room – all windows on one side. I requested round tables. I have been so excited about it.

I feel embarrassed to ask people to pay for their own meals. It reminds me of the cartoon Popeye. There was a character named Wimpy. He was always saying, "Come for duck dinner. You bring the duck!"

Lots of love,

Mom

Chapter 6 – 1999

January 1, 1999

Dear Elaine and Alex,

It's been a long time since I wrote to you, but I feel that I have an acceptable reason. My eyes have been giving me fits – and still are. I'm sitting here now typing with my eyes closed.

I'm glad Christmas is over. I have said that it should be called "Mama's Day." Mama buys and wraps the presents. Mama buys and addresses the cards. Mama gets to prepare and serve the food. Mama gets to clean up and put it all away when everyone goes home. This mama has usually had more than enough fun by the time it is over.

I'm anticipating getting things around for the birthday party. I'm going to go in to Perkins soon and talk to Renee again about the arrangements. I have been inviting people like crazy and now have thirty-one coming to the dinner.

You asked if you should stay in town. As I told you, I'd love to have you stay here. I have constantly debated about my advice on the subject. I am prejudiced in favor of your staying here, but I love you enough to wonder if you'd want to. The upstairs is cold, but I can take up the little electric heater.

The big negative is that Quentin still wets the bed at night. I have purchased those blue pads and have them next to the mattress, on top of the mattress pad and on the bed under the rubberized pad. I put one or two on the floor under the walker where I park the urinal. This morning the bed was wet. The pads and wet pajamas were on the carpet (not on a blue pad). Several nights last week he missed the urinal altogether.

The fact that you have to go through our bedroom to get to the shower is probably reason enough to stay at a motel in town.

I was really down yesterday. The situation hasn't changed any, but I'm looking at it differently today. It is easy to get real disgusted – one could even say real, real disgusted. This morning I had the thought that this is not the Quentin I loved for so many years. It is hard to remember now how careful he used to be. He never came in the house with dirty boots. He never went over the white carpet wearing boots or dirty clothes. He always took his work clothes off in the little bathroom. He always hung up his clothes. He was real particular about the way they were hung in the closet – the work clothes were first, with everything facing the same direction.

He had good table manners and read the Time magazine from cover to cover, as well as the Farm Journal, Successful Farming, the High Plains Journal and the Hutchinson News. He kept up on the news and current events. I was always proud to be his wife. When he was with people, he laughed and joked and was a good guy. He was exactly the same at home.

I think it is understandable that I go through some days when I feel very burdened. Thank goodness for faith! I try to always remember and to be thankful that he still has a good disposition and a sense of humor. He appreciates me and tells me so almost every day. As long as I have my mind and the ability to read and think, I will get along fine. Sometimes it takes an attitude adjustment. I also have a selfish motive for staying positive. I don't want to end up as a semi-invalid with lots of aches and pains when this is over.

I'm glad to know you two always bring good weather with you when you travel. Yesterday we had a freezing mist and then a little snow all day. The sun is shining today, but the temperature was 13 when I checked earlier.

We finished breakfast at 10:00 this morning. We had oatmeal, orange juice, bananas, toast and coffee. I wasn't hungry at noon, but at 12:30 Quentin could see the time on the clock and he wanted to eat lunch. We had soup.

Lots of love,

Madelyn

January 23, 1999

Dear Elaine & Alex,

This is mostly to tell you how much we enjoyed having you here for the birthday party. We are very pleased with the way everything went. The other day I commented, "Well, the party is over, so I can get on to something else."

Quentin replied, "The party isn't over for me. I will be thinking about it for a long time." I feel good about that. I bought a nice scrapbook in town yesterday to put all of the cards in, and I wrote a thank you to put in the paper. I was surprised that it cost $13.50. Quentin said I had written too much. I didn't feel that I had. I have written a long one for the church and have turned it in. That newsletter will be printed next week.

Have enjoyed the Christmas presents – am using up my little dabs of perfume before I open your gift. Love the Cuddle Duds, and I love the globe. I have located all the islands where Quentin was stationed during The War and have located other places, too. I told your kids that I was geographically illiterate, so this will help. It was so thoughtful of them to get it for us.

Will write more later.

Lots of love,

Mom

February 9, 1999

Dear Elaine and Alex,

The kitchen has been given a good cleaning, brown rice is in the microwave cooking, Quentin is asleep, I have a Diet Pepsi on a coaster in front of me, so I can write you the past due letter.

I'm hoping he will get excited enough about the possibility of going to St. Louis for the reunion of the 13th Air Force that he'll try to get stronger. Larry and I were in the garage yesterday, and I told him that I didn't think Quentin was walking as well. He agreed with me. I told Quentin that if he gets down completely, I will have to sell some land and put him in a nursing home. It didn't bother him at all. I'm sure he figures that he will commit suicide so he won't have to go. I had Larry take his gun away at least three years ago. Quentin hasn't discovered it's gone.

He failed the driving test to get his license renewed. He didn't come to a complete stop at two stop signs and swerved over the median line more than once. Christy asked if the instructor was white-knuckled when they got back. He told me the other day he was going to drive over to Conway. Of course, I told him that he couldn't, as he doesn't have a license.

Christy came over with the cutest little dog. She said he was very expensive, but they wanted a dog. They had borrowed money to finish the basement, but they ran out before getting the carpet, so the rest of that job is on hold. I refrained from saying that the money for the dog would have gone a long way toward purchasing the carpet. I haven't managed to stop thinking sharp thoughts, but I have learned to keep my mouth shut. For a while I was thinking about getting a cat or a dog. It was a time of brief insanity from which I have recovered.

I am pleased about your volunteer work. I have read a number of times how good it is for a person to do volunteer work and how they live longer. I have always loved the volunteer work I have done and enjoyed the people involved. When I was active in the hospital auxiliary and I'd see a pink smock in the grocery store, I would immediately think, "I see a friend!"

Lots of love,

Madelyn

February 17, 1999

Dear Elaine and Alex,

I'm going to have to talk fast. It is almost time for Quentin to inform me he wants to get ready for bed. However, he slept all morning and is feeling pretty good now, so if his book is good enough he will "read" for a while.

I enjoyed the final draft of the story you sent. I read it to Quentin. He still didn't think you would get any special notice from that story. I have enclosed the book, *Bird by Bird* by Ann LaMont. I have read it twice. She had some advice that sounded good to me. However, I found her language unacceptable. There have been so many movies where the emphasis is on "being real." I can do without watching people talk while brushing their teeth, seeing men using a urinal in a public restroom, or watching a couple barely covered obviously having sex.

I'm glad that I don't aspire to being published. I think a person could describe all of my letters as being "shitty first drafts." If I don't get a letter in the mail immediately, I think of a lot of ways to change it. Someday I'm going to write down the experience of having the wheat field catch on fire. I don't have time for that now, but I think it should be preserved in more than just memory. I do appreciate your sending the first drafts and the finished copy of all your stories.

My eyes are much better. I've had the wax cleaned out of my ears and am hearing better, but it still isn't right. It is absolutely horrible to not be able to hear. A friend called on Sunday night and was trying to give me a name that I had asked her for, and she finally said she would write to me.

I saw a new book at the library the other night written by Joseph Girzone entitled *A Portrait of Jesus*. I started reading it to Quentin last night, and he seemed to like it.

Speaking of books, Irving Sone wrote *The Agony and the Ecstasy*, which would make the paintings of Michelangelo in Italy more meaningful for you. It starts with Michelangelo as a boy and goes on through his tempestuous career. I think it would be wonderful background reading for your trip. I love to read – can be terribly tired and sit down and read for a while and feel invigorated.

We discovered we had 83 bushels of soybeans still in storage so we sold them. I suggested we cash the check and start a fund to go to Quentin's 13th Air Force Reunion in St. Louis. Quentin wisely said it would be better to send the money to the bank. Besides, he said the trip to St. Louis was iffy. I've tried to tell him that if he would exercise and walk better he might not even need the scooter. I tell him he is lazy and all kinds of things to make him more ambitious, but have not had a lot of luck motivating him.

I have been meditating, doing Reiki and listening to Mozart morning and evening. I have been feeling great and have a lot of energy. I like the tape you folks gave us the best of all. I have listened to it over and over, but would probably not recognize it if I were to hear it someplace else. Jean and I are alike in that way, unfortunately. She said she can always recognize the Star Spangled Banner because people stand up. That sounds funny, but it really isn't that far-fetched for people who are as deaf to music as we are.

Lots of love,

Madelyn

March 9, 1999

Dear Elaine and Alex,

This is another cold, dreary day. It was 27 when I got up. It had only warmed up to 28 two hours later. We didn't go to the Y. Quentin doesn't like coming out from the pool in cold weather. I could have gone without him, but I have a lot of letters to write. I've been thinking of a statement I read in a Unity publication years ago. "My heart makes its own weather, and my heart says it is spring."

I was reminded of that on the trip to Salina yesterday. The trees, wheat and some flowers have decided it is time for spring, in spite of cold weather, snow and freezing rain.

I decided that I am rather enjoying this weather. As soon as it warms up and spring is actually here, it will mean I will have to get out in the yard. I have been pushing since Christmas, so it is nice to have an empty calendar right now. I like to get up in the morning, put on my make-up and something decent to wear so I'm ready to go in case someone should call and make a good offer.

We heard from Quentin's Air Force buddy today. Quentin told me an interesting story this morning that he had never bothered with (or thought about) before. Rabb had a chance to fly to Australia during the war. He had some friends in Sidney and he stayed in their home. It seems they had a daughter who wanted to come to the United States real bad. When Rabb went to bed, he found her in the bed naked. If we go to the reunion in St. Louis it will be interesting to see if Rabb's wife has an Australian accent.

I have decided to ask all of you to write down the memories you have of your dad and to keep them. I'm going to be doing it too. Maybe they could be pooled for a eulogy – or just kept for private memories. It's hard sometimes to remember the man he used to be. I have no illusions now about his getting better. I thank God for his good disposition and the traces of the original Quentin that I see sometimes. Right now he could be described as being lazy and repulsive. I don't want to have to wait several years for the good memories from the past to resurface.

Yesterday I started setting the alarm clock and putting it at the other end of the table where he has to get up to shut it off. I've told him to walk around the circle of rooms and go to the bathroom. The alarm went off a little while ago, and he did get up and turn it off, but he didn't do any extra walking – probably didn't go to the bathroom either. He gets interested in a book and forgets all about going to the bathroom.

One reason I wanted to go to Salina yesterday was to get some of the waterproof underpants from Target. I was so provoked the other day – there is no other brand that has the elastic top like the ones from Target. I mentally composed a letter to Depends berating them for not having that kind. I'm going to call Depends' toll free customer number and tell them what I think of their product.

I am of the opinion that whoever dreams up these awful things has never had to help someone get into one. I am going to suggest that some of the young, able-bodied men try wearing one.

He has reached a stage I never expected. He watches the TV ads as if they are the most interesting thing in the world. That is very aggravating to me when he's watching the ads and loads his spoon over-full and dribbles it to his mouth. I can't understand how he can sit around in his pajamas with his bare butt sticking out for hours. He would let it hang out all day if I didn't command him to pull his pants up. This morning when I was fussing with him, he told me to get something to put over him, which I wouldn't do. I made him stand up, and then I pulled them up for him. I think I gave him what the kids call a "wedgy".

Saturday

I got delayed with the letter writing. Had one of the "spells" with my eyes the other day. I had gone to the library and all of a sudden, the left eye starting burning and watering. I carry some drops in my purse, so I put them in while I was in the library. I got through checking out my books and tapes and hurried to the car. Had to sit there for quite a while before I could drive. I felt like crying! My eyes are very precious to me. I don't know what caused this infection in the tear ducts, but it sure has been miserable.

I get a monthly newsletter from Dr. Weil, which is called *The Bottom Line*. I like it, as it has information from doctors as well as from well-known people in the alternative medicine field. I found a nugget of information the other day about high blood pressure. It stated that high blood pressure can be hereditary, or it can come from hidden emotions!

These emotions can cause problems in the blood that can lead to strokes or heart attacks – especially if a person gets very tired. That is the only explanation for stroke that I have read that makes sense in Quentin's case. He had been so terribly tired all season, and I scolded him for working so hard.

He had already officially retired – supposedly. My thinking was that he might as well have been getting the money since he was working so hard. He said Larry was taking all the responsibility, so he didn't mind just taking a small hourly wage. He had the stroke two days after the fall harvest was finished.

It is really snowing now. Last night it looked like an incoming fog before I went to bed. Early this morning everything was covered with snow. It has been coming down heavy with huge flakes for over an hour now. They have forecast up to 14 inches – we could do with a lot less than that!

I'm going to hurry out to the mail box with this letter and hope the mailman and I get there at about the same time.

Lots of love,

Mom

March 19, 1999

Dear Elaine and Alex,

I'm going to start this letter and hope my eyes hold up long enough to get it finished. They are much better, but still not back to normal.

I had something I wanted to tell you that isn't very good telephone conversation. I am in training for a position that will pay from $36,000 to $48,000 a year! Sounds pretty good, doesn't it? It isn't glamorous, and it won't be any fun. I have made the decision that I absolutely will not put Quentin in a nursing home unless he gets in such a condition – or I do – that I just cannot take care of him any longer.

At our last Fellowship meeting one woman said she admired me so much for what I was doing. Her husband had been in a nursing home, which was supposed to be a good one in Great Bend. He was getting such poor care that she finally took him home for the last three months of his life. She said, "I HATE NURSING HOMES! I HATE NURSING HOMES!"

It was just a few days later that Harold Hanson died. He had been in the Bethany Home in Lindsborg, which is considered a very good one. However, it seems that every time Harold had a serious problem, Opal was the one who had to alert the staff.

Why should I pay out that kind of money to go sit in the nursing home and still have to be the primary caregiver? Our home is fixed up good for an invalid. I could also hire home health care. If cooking gets to be a problem, there are all kinds of things already prepared. It would mean that our expenses would escalate from the present level, but there would be lots of advantages besides the money. I can't think of anything more exhausting than going to a nursing home every day and sitting there from morning to night.

If Quentin gets to the point that he's in a semi-conscience state, he would sleep a lot, and that would actually give me some freedom. I could also get better and more housekeeping help and still be money ahead. I spent enough time with Grandpa Stan and my parents in nursing homes to last me a lifetime.

I sat down with Quentin last night and told him what I had decided. He said, "You just added ten years to my life." I didn't tell him that I sure hoped not! And I don't!

I was in the library recently and saw an interesting new book entitled *Why People Don't Heal – And How They Can,* by Caroline Myss, Ph.D. There was one sentence that has really helped me. She said a person had to take a *detached* attitude. I have been working on doing that.

I got along real well Sunday and Monday, but for some reason, I didn't master it yesterday. For one thing, I was going to Hutch to have my hearing aids cleaned and I suggested Quentin go along. He wanted to. I had a 2:00 o'clock appointment, so I rushed lunch and the dishes and told Quentin I had to use eye drops and lie down for a short time. I got up at 1:20, and he was still sitting in the chair without his socks and shoes on. I was not real detached about that.

He got himself to the car without his mints or cane. I didn't go back in to get either one. On the way to Hutch he said he liked me the way I had been on Sunday and Monday much better.

I told him I had not signed any contract to take care of

him and that I could and would back out of this deal if he didn't help a little. We were going to the pool this morning, so I told him at 8:30 that he had to shave and put his clothes on over his swimming suit. We leave here by 10:30. I figured that ought to give him enough time.

Later I went to check on him, and he was sitting in his swimming trunks in the bathroom. He said he couldn't go. He looked terrible, so I asked if he didn't feel well. He was having trouble with loose bowels, so I agreed that he didn't need to go. I have been real nice to him today and have the detached business under control.

One thing that upset me so yesterday was that as he was putting his coat on he was almost on his knees. That brought out the meanness in me and I told him very nicely (?) that I hoped he didn't get the knees of his pants too dirty getting to the car. In reading ads about nursing homes they all talk about the loving care they give patients. Sometimes I have thought he might get more loving care in a home. Will work diligently on detaching myself from the rather small aggravations, and have decided that I just can't get provoked when it takes him five or ten minutes, or even a couple hours, to move himself.

Lots of love,

Madelyn

March 25,

Dear Elaine and Alex,

My day didn't start off with a detached attitude this morning. I walked barefooted to the bathroom and stepped into a big, wet puddle adjacent to the pad on the floor under the walker. That makes me so damned mad! He was doing so well for a while, and I told him I sure appreciated it.

That was still better than yesterday. I had to wash the blankets, sheet, underpads – everything. He smelled so bad that I told him to take a shower. I got a lot done waiting for him. It took almost 45 minutes. He was so sleepy all morning that he fell asleep at the table, so I got him back to bed. I know from past experience that stroke victims are very difficult to cope with. When they look the same and act almost the same a great deal of the time, it is difficult to understand on days when they are "out of it." I'm grateful he's not in a lot of pain, even though I think pain might be easier to understand than mental deterioration.

Have been thinking how nice it was when we were in Florida. As we were eating breakfast and would see someone mowing the lawn, we would comment, "It must be Tuesday."

I loved going out in the morning and seeing that the flowers in front of the apartment had been watered. Also, I'll never forget Valentine's Day, 1993 when we were in

Port Richy, Florida. We had gone to an inspirational early church service. We were on our way to meet Jean and Frank and another couple at a very elegant country club.

On the way, we stopped at a grocery store to see if we could find an inexpensive floral gift for Jean and her friend. We were about to give up when the clerk showed us an orchid mounted in a small white wicker basket. We selected two. I must have been looking wistful, because Quentin asked if I would like to have one. I said I sure would!

It was so pretty that I didn't want to mess up the corsage by wearing it, so I kept it in the basket. Our meal was delicious. There was free champagne and a flower for each lady. As we drove around that day I had the most joyous awareness of how much I loved my husband of fifty-one years. The flower lasted three weeks. This is another experience I will never be able to duplicate.

It is almost noon and I have been writing long enough that the mailman has received the message and will certainly hurry to get the mail delivered early in an effort to thwart me.

Lots of love,

Madelyn

March 29, 1999

Dear Elaine and Alex,

My resolution and thought today is that I'm going to be very active in promoting good health and stamina in myself so I can take care of Quentin. I am aware that it has to be spiritual as well as physical. I will continue to give Quentin the best help possible. Sometimes I think he will probably live to be 90.

I have said from the beginning that this is an opportunity for growth. Have to admit at times it has been a struggle and I have not progressed. After developing arthritic like pain in my fingers and thumbs, I realized I needed to take a spiritual and mental inventory of myself. There are a number of good things I can think about and be thankful for:

- Quentin still has his wonderful disposition and traces of his sense of humor.
- He is appreciative of what I do for him, and he tells me so. He also tells me that he loves me.
- He does try to please me.
- He can get involved with his talking book and doesn't care what I do.

The Trying Traits:

- He gets so involved with a book that he forgets to go to the bathroom.
- He sits around for hours in his pajamas with his

bare butt sticking out.

- He refuses to take any responsibility for his physical improvement.
- Watching him almost crawl when he walks with his knees bent makes me crazy.
- His slowness in getting motivated to get dressed – or get moving in any way.
- His terribly sloppy table manners.

As I have thought today about this situation, I am aware it could be much worse. As I think about a nursing home, I have put it in dollars and cents. By keeping him at home, I am earning at least $36,000 a year – which is pretty good for a 75 year-old woman.

By having him at home, I can still have my own life. The thoughts of spending hours every day in a nursing home is most unappealing. Another dollar and cents benefit is that I can save the ground, which would mean an adequate income for me and would leave an inheritance for all you kids. Don't know how much more incentive I could have or need.

I'm going to focus on the affirmation, "God is healing all now. Thank you, God."

Love,

Mom

April 2, 1999

Dear Elaine and Alex,

We skipped church on Sunday because Quentin had a horrible headache. He had a big crying spell – couldn't understand why he'd felt good all week and had to get sick on Sunday. Later Larry took him for a ride, which seemed to help his attitude. I started in again on the book, *Why Some People Don't Heal and What You Can do About It.*

I have focused on maintaining a detached attitude. I'm going to try harder to stay detached about his table manners and other little things that are bothering me. I will concentrate on his good qualities, such as his disposition and appreciation for me.

Not everyone who has had a stroke has those traits. A lot of men who have never suffered a stroke don't even have those qualities. I'm also going to learn to meditate while he is playing his tapes. There is no point or virtue in both of us losing our health. Quentin has a wonderful opportunity to let go of sex and work and replace them with spiritual knowledge. I am willing to help him in the quest, and I am willing to develop spiritually. I will take the steps as I'm guided.

Lots of love,

Mom

April 4, 1999

Hello Everybody!

This is a beautiful Easter day. I didn't get to church this morning and was sorry, as I had planned on going. Have not missed very many Easter Sunday church services in my many years of living. I was so tired and sleepy this morning that I didn't have the energy to get ready.

Quentin awakened me at 5:00 a.m. this morning by falling out of bed. I could not get him to do anything that would make it possible for me to hoist him back up in bed. I finally gave up, got a pillow and a blanket for him, left him on the floor and I went back to bed. I told him I would call Larry when I was sure he would be awake. I don't know how long it was before he got smart enough to get himself up on the bed.

Guess I had better go back and give you a little history about his recent episode. He got up Monday morning barely able to get around. I thought his trouble was because he doesn't do anything except sit at the table and listen to his books, so I was determined we were going to the Y. It was with great difficulty that I got him motivated and dressed. At one time he said, "I will drown." I lovingly told him if he started to drown I wouldn't holler for help.

In the afternoon he had some chest pains a couple different times, but they didn't last long and weren't severe. That night he was on the floor twice. He fell out of bed about 3:00 a.m. and again at 5:00. The first time he was lying north and south at the foot of the bed. He would sit up and then fall back down again. I put my knees up against his back to keep him supported and told him to scoot. Every time he moved I moved with him holding him all the time with my legs. He finally got over far enough that I could use the hoist to get him back into bed. The second time he rolled out of bed I got up and we went through the same procedure.

When we were having our "treat" time about 4:00 that same day, he had a very sharp chest pain. He made a face and put his hand on his chest. I asked if it were severe and he said it was. In just a little bit he said it had moved to the other side but wasn't severe. I had a feeling that we could very well end up in the hospital, so I had him go in and take a shower. He hadn't had a shower for two days and smelled awful!

We waited for Larry to get home, get cleaned up and have a bite to eat. Quentin could barely walk. If it hadn't been for Larry, I would have had to call an ambulance, as I would not have been able to get him to the car.

He had wonderful care when he got to the hospital. Larry helped the technician hold Quentin up so they could take chest and stomach X-rays. The lab technician came and took a lot of blood. When the doctor came in he said that Quentin was full of poop, for one thing. They said it was also possible that Quentin had had a small stroke. Anyhow, they admitted him. It was after 11:00 before I left the hospital.

I had the feeling the nurses would not have objected to my staying longer, but I was terribly tired and hungry. I couldn't think of anything else I needed to do for Quentin, but I could think of a number of things I needed to do for myself.

On Wednesday morning they did more blood work and a brain scan. Quentin was terribly weak and discouraged. They had given him a big shot of Milk of Magnisia, and it had worked. When I got there he was struggling to get from the bathroom to the bed and he cried (as he does frequently). He said he didn't know why he couldn't have died when he was 80. The rest of the day went fairly well.

On Thursday the doctor came in and said the brain scan was good and most of the blood tests were okay. He does have a prostate infection again, though. The therapist came to work with him that morning. I was so thrilled. He walked amazingly well and followed her instructions for the simple exercises. She told him she would be back in the afternoon. Quentin's face looked like he used to – alive and alert. I was happy when he said, "I'm eighty, but I'm not going to let that stop me."

I practically floated home at lunch time. I went back

in the afternoon and he was back to being what has become normal for him – despondent and uncooperative. When the therapist came back Quentin only walked a little ways, and he didn't respond at all to the exercises.

I had dressed so I could go directly from the hospital to the Maundy Thursday service at the hospital. I did go out to Sirloin Stockade and had a delicious meal, as I had been eating a lot of quick, short meals. I went back to the hospital to say goodnight, and he was so depressed that I stayed with him until the nurse came to give him a bath. He was dismissed Friday morning and has shown no signs of returning to "the good old days."

I had decided last week that I could take care of him and not put him in a nursing home. I figured I could get home health care and housekeeping services and get by fine. This episode has shown me that there could well be a time, in the not too distant future, when I might have to put him in a home. There is no way I can handle him if he can't get up and move a little bit. I do think he may have had another small stroke. His speech is worse, and I don't think his mind is as good. I will take care of him as long as I possibly can. However, there is no point in my getting down and being in worse shape than he is.

I have been focusing on "detaching myself from the situation." It has spared me a lot of negative energy. I guess I was plenty detached this morning when he was down on the floor and I gave him a pillow and covered him with a blanket. That's the first time in my life I have ever done anything like that.

I want to get this in the mail, and I'm going to have to hurry. I'm making copies of this letter, as I would say the same thing to everyone anyhow, and I just don't have the time.

Love all of you and appreciate you!

Lots of love,

Madelyn

April 7, 1999

Dear Elaine and Alex

I think Quentin did have another stroke. I'm having more trouble understanding him, and it is a mess to try to get him motivated. Took three hours to get him to the bathroom to take a shower, get dressed and do a half-assed job of shaving and brushing his teeth.

We were fifteen minutes late getting to his therapy appointment. I am taking him to town later to get his $100 prescription, and we will go to the park and walk a few feet. Hope I can get him in the pool tomorrow. I got him up there yesterday but he wouldn't get out of the car. I find this very trying!

Thank you for the Easter card and message. I'm so glad you are coming home in May, Elaine. I definitely think he had another stroke. I had hoped it was a bad case of depression – that would be easier to overcome.

Later

I just got home from town. I had to get a new print cartridge so I could print out your letter. Earlier this morning I wrote this particular piece more or less for myself. I thought you might be interested, so I'm sending it on to you.

Someone asked recently how I visualized God. I have never been able to answer that, although I have been aware of God since I was a child. At a very early age, He was someone who watched and could see everything. He was a God who punished.

In my teens, I couldn't believe God was as revengeful toward women as I had been taught. As I was lying in bed this morning, in a half-awake, half-asleep stage and in a peaceful state, I started thinking about God. I received these thoughts:

God is Spirit without form, but very real.

God is like the wind, which is felt but not seen.

God is like light. We see light as the absence of darkness, but neither one can be held, measured or analyzed.

God is like heat and cold. We can experience both and think of it coming from a concrete source – a stove, furnace, burning objects or the weather. We also consider cold as coming from the weather, refrigerator, freezer, etc. Actually, God has been the original source and has inspired people to find, use, and expand the natural resources that have been here from the beginning – just as his spirit is within us as our very life.

In the beginning of Biblical history, God chose to reveal Himself and stated that man was created in His image and that He breathed the life into him/her. Then people started creating God in *their* own image. When things had become such a terrible mess, Jesus was sent to show us what God was like in the human form. It was as if God decided His own image had become so distorted that he needed to correct it. That was the reason Jesus came to us in human form – to show us how God could be understood and expressed in our individual lives. Jesus attributed his life and works to God and expressed His love, compassion and guidance.

I thanked God for showing me these truths. I have never before been able to state these feelings, as they were nebulous. I have never had the understanding of Jesus that I have desired and prayed for. I think I may have made a big spiritual leap. I will continue to pray for guidance in my every day life as I care for Quentin, manage our money and relationships with family and friends. I am also praying for all of God's children who are suffering from war, poverty, and bad relationships.

I felt lighter somehow, after writing this down. I'll be interested in your reaction. I don't know if this is something that can be shared, or if each person's understanding of God and relationship with Him is totally individualized.

Gotta go.

Lots of love,

Madelyn

April 12, 1999

Dear Elaine and Alex,

Quentin is sound asleep in bed, but I will try to awaken him in about an hour. Yesterday afternoon we stretched out to take a nap. I had put a pad on the bed and pulled the spread over us. I had the urinal by the bed and a pad on the floor. Quentin awoke from the nap, managed to sit on the spread – off of the pad – and let go. He must have urinated a gallon. Everything was wet down to the final pad. I got him to the dining room at 3:00 o'clock, gave him a clean pad and clean pants and told him to put them on.

Marg came at 5:00 and he was still sitting there wearing nothing but a shirt. She said, "Quentin, you aren't wearing any pants!" Didn't bother him. He said, "You won't see much." He was slumped over, so I don't think he was "flashing" her.

After I had done all of our ritual last night – put on the Breathe-Rite Strip, given him Vicks to put in his nose, did his Reiki treatment, and kissed him goodnight – I said that I hoped he'd feel better in the morning. His comment was that he did too, or that God would take him.

When I woke up this morning he was not in bed. I figured he was in the dining room, so I didn't hurry to get out of bed. When I did get up he was sitting on the stool all stooped over. I went to the other bathroom and emptied the urinal. I told him I was going to put clean clothes out for him. When I came out of the bathroom he was back in bed and could hardly hold his eyes open. He wanted to know if he had kept the bed dry. He had. Bless his heart. I have no idea how long he was in the bathroom. I know he was afraid of waking me up and didn't know what the condition of the bed would be.

I feel I am making great progress spiritually. Had an encouraging thought last night. If life had not been as it has in the past five years, I probably would not have had the incentive to grow spiritually.

At this stage my prayer is, "I release Quentin into Your care, and if Your will is for him to stay alive, I pray we will be guided to use the time for spiritual growth. I accept Your guidance in what I need to do. Thank you, God."

I appreciate your love and concern, but I hope you

won't worry about me too much. I am a fairly decent person, but have never been a doormat. Have had times when I did a lot of crying (maybe some kicking and screaming) and have had to do some hard things, but with God's help I have always come through it. I intend to this time. Maybe sometime I will learn enough that I won't have to keep going through these rougher times. That would be nice!

Well, Quentin is up now and is very dense. I gave him a glass of prune juice and made a piece of toast to hold him for an hour. I helped him put on the pad, and he has instructions to put on his pants, but I doubt he has done it yet. Had better go take care of him.

Thanks for being good listeners! We are looking forward to having you come, Elaine.

Lots of love,

Mom

April 13, 1999

Dear Elaine and Alex,

Quentin slept well last night – didn't fall out of bed until this morning. As usual, he scooted around in an impossible position. I let the hoist down and told him to get up to the left side of the bed so I could help him up. I went in the bathroom, closed the door and got dressed. When I came out he was in the dining room in his wet clothes. I got a dry pad and pants out. I did help him put on his shirt. He just sat there without moving.

I finally told him he would not get any breakfast until he was dressed. I fixed mine, sat down and ate it. I was almost through by the time he got dressed, so I went ahead and finished. As the saying goes, "There's more than one way to skin a cat."

Teri said if the doctor would prescribe therapy at home that Medicare will pay for it. When I told Quentin about that, he said and he didn't think we needed any more help. He said the new cleaning lady should be able to provide the extra help I need. I told him the kids were all concerned about me and that I was constantly being asked about a nursing home. He acted like he didn't hear me.

I'll keep you posted.

April 19, 1999

Hello Everybody,

This is another letter to bring you up to date on the situation here. Had a call from Dr. Larzalere this morning saying that Quentin's PSA test was up to 117. Two weeks ago it was 86.7. Quentin is very concerned about it. I am too. He has resisted having prostate surgery for five years, and he is at the stage now where he doesn't want any surgery. He wants to die.

However, we don't want the cancer spreading to his

bones. Teri offered to go with us tomorrow to see the urologist in Salina. I will probably accept her offer. It is good to have better ears than mine. My mind tends to go on hold when the doctor starts talking, especially when the options are not pleasant.

Quentin is going to start getting therapy at home. The nurse who came to evaluate him has also prescribed bathing help for two weeks. The nurse from the Double A Health Care came out Thursday afternoon and spent about an hour-and-a- half evaluating Quentin and looking at our care facilities. She was very impressed with the hoist – thought it was ingenious.

I know everyone has been concerned about me, and I appreciate the love and caring. I do feel that I am handling the situation quite well. I have sort of a detached attitude about the whole thing, which is a big help. I try to be as loving and helpful as I can be, but I'm not getting terribly emotional about everything. I take at least an hour after I get Quentin to bed at night and another hour in the morning for exercises and meditation. It helps. I should have been keeping a journal all these years. It would be interesting now to see the many stages I have gone through. It has taken many years to get to this place of detached peace and acceptance. Thank God for this place!

I called our minister this morning and told him he could activate the prayer chain. I'm praying the doctor will make the right decision for what is best for Quentin. I continue to pray that if it is God's will, he can be released from this world.

I hope you don't mind getting a common letter. I just don't have the time right now to write individual letters. Thanks for the support and love and prayers we receive from all of you.

Lots of love,

Madelyn

April 25, 1999

Dear Elaine and Alex,

Hope the weather clears up by the time you get here – before even. There is water standing everywhere, and we've had days of gray, cloudy, drizzly weather. I would enjoy some sunshine. Larry was here for a while tonight. He said his mood is affected by this kind of weather. I have been rather cross today, so guess the weather, or something else is getting to me, too.

My load has been easier lately. I've been double diapering Quentin, and I've told him to not even try to get up in the night. Haven't had any wet sheets, blankets or carpets for a few days. He has been awfully tired in the evenings after therapy, and that causes him to be real dull.

I have had to help him get dressed and undressed for some time, but it is getting worse. I asked the therapist if

I should help or if I should leave him alone to struggle through it. She said he should do as much as possible for himself, but there would be times when I needed to help. I think he is very happy to have me help. He likes it better than doing it himself.

I had an interesting day on Friday. I went to coffee, as usual. As we were leaving we saw the minister from the Episcopal Church walk past the window. I've heard that he is dying of bone cancer. I went out and introduced myself to him and told him we were praying for him. I told him my husband's prostate cancer had become active. I said I hoped I wasn't being too personal, but I wondered if his cancer had started in his prostate. He said his cancer started in his lung.

He has just finished six weeks of radiation. He said it only took ten minutes, but was a "damned nuisance". He has started chemotherapy now. The doctor said that bone cancer was extremely painful. It isn't like arthritis, which comes and goes.

I commented to him that I didn't know how a person lived without faith. I was shocked when he made a comment about God, and then said, "If there is a God."

I wish we had been inside where it was warm. I think we could have had an even more interesting conversation. We talked about how we had changed because of the illnesses. He said he and his wife have developed a greater sense of humor. They see things funny that I guess most people wouldn't. I told him I had developed a detached attitude. He says he calls it "creative indifference" and he has developed too. I like it better, as "detached" seems cold. Whatever you call it, it means not being emotionally ravaged by the progression of events.

I have been praying for him and thinking how hard it would be to preach every Sunday if a person doubted God. He made an additional statement that just came to me. He said it makes a person feel better to believe something is out there. It sounds as if he is not aware of the fact that God is present within us and not "out there."

Looking forward so very much to having you, Elaine. Hope the weather warms up so we can sit on the porch and talk. I have always enjoyed our night-time visits so much. There were a lot of times when we sure would have enjoyed the porch. Remember how cold it was at times – and how windy?

We loved your story *How Francis Got His Wink*. There aren't many love stories written about old people. I've read it to Quentin several times, and every time he just cries and cries, but he wants to hear it again. We are both excited that you are getting this one published.

Having the new cleaning lady sure takes a burden off of me. The home therapy has also been a tremendous help. They will start giving Quentin bathing help next

Tuesday. I was told they will also cut his toenails and fingernails and help with shaving if necessary.

Quentin rode the bicycle for at least twenty minutes this afternoon without my having to threaten him. I can't see a lot of improvement in his walking, but I have hopes. It used to worry me so thinking that if he got down I would have no choice for his care. I have hopes now that we can avoid the nursing home route.

Alex, I know you will miss Elaine when she's here. Hope something interesting develops for you. This won't be a real fun trip for her. It certainly won't compare to any of the trips you two take together, but it does mean a lot to both of us.

Lots of love,

Mom

July 6, 1999

Dear Elaine and Alex,

This is the first morning since June 4 that I have not gone to town early. I'm so tired I feel as if I can't move. It has helped to have Quentin at Angel Arms. The people who run the home health care company also manage this facility. As I told you, it is not a full-care nursing home, but they do have skilled people to watch out for him and they are all very kind.

I'm afraid you are going hate it. His room is practically in the hallway, and it feels so exposed. Hopefully, he will recover quickly and we'll be able to bring him back home before long. Until then, I'm changing my schedule. I'm going to try to get some rest and build up my own strength. I've decided I'm not going to go in there until after the mail comes. I will stay with Quentin until supper time, and then I'll come home.

Jennifer was here yesterday. Danny and Ady will be here sometime this week, and Christy is always great about coming to visit. We sure had fun with your kids a few days ago. They wanted to take us out to lunch, but I didn't want them to spend a lot of money on us. Our minister had told us about a wonderful new barbeque place. We went there and got sandwiches to go, and it cost less than $9.00. (Quentin had already eaten.)

We decided to go to Lakeside Park and have a picnic. There is a pair of white swans, and they have two babies. (Swans are very territorial.)

I had brought Pepsi from home, and I'd gone to the car to get it. I heard a bunch of squawking, and when I turned around I saw Eric had the male swan by the neck. I yelled at him to not hurt the swan. Everyone started laughing hysterically. The swan had gone after Quentin while I wasn't looking. Evidently he didn't like the scooter. He started pecking at Quentin's leg, so Eric went up and grabbed him around the neck to pull him away. I screamed when I saw it. I thought Eric was choking him.

Eric eventually got the swan back to the water. I now understand the saying "ruffled feathers." The swan reminded me of a longshoreman. His feathers were all fluffed out, his head stuck out in a belligerent manner and he walked slowly and deliberately, as if he were threatening and saying, "Stay away from my woman!"

Of course, Eric egged him on, and that just made matters worse. Quentin laughed so hard that tears rolled down his cheeks. I wish I had thought to bring my camera. We had such a good time. I had forgotten how good it feels to laugh.

I'm going to take a nap before I head back to town. I'll keep you posted.

Lots of love,

Mom

July 14, 1999

Dear Elaine and Alex,

For some time now, I have been praying for Quentin's release from this world – if it was God's will. If not, then I prayed that we would learn the spiritual lessons we were supposed to learn.

Yesterday, Quentin was in very bad condition physically. I sat, holding his hand, thinking every breath would be his last. The nurse came in around mid-morning and asked if I wanted to send him to the hospital. After a pause, I told her this was a terrible decision to make, but no.

Even after they put him on oxygen he was having a hard time breathing. The minister came in and was appalled. He said something could be done for Quentin's pain, and he was adamant that we should send him to the hospital. I agreed to it because I was afraid he was really suffering. The doctor knew how we felt, so he ordered no "blue code" when he called for an ambulance.

Quentin was in ventricle cardiac fibrillation. This morning the doctor told me he had suffered a stroke and a heart attack and there was a spot on his lung. They are going to x-ray him again tomorrow to learn what is causing it. Yesterday his mind was bad and his speech incoherent. By this evening he was talking well and seemed more lucid until he got upset about the giant spiders he saw crawling up the wall. He got very agitated when I couldn't see them. He said they were as big as dinner plates. I think it's the pain medication that's causing him to hallucinate.

I've had a hard time dealing with my guilt. I was so tired the night he fell that I couldn't think or move. Plus, I was mad at him. I don't know why he insisted on getting up in the middle of the night and stumbling around in the dark trying to use the bathroom when he was content to sit at the dining room table and wet his pants all day long while listening to his talking books.

I didn't even consider the fact that he might be seriously hurt. He had fallen out of bed and slipped off the side of it so many times that it wasn't a big deal for him to be on the floor. He'd never fallen very hard or very far, and the biggest problem had always been getting him back up.

I didn't want to call Larry and get him up in the middle of the night. He's always desperately tired from the heat and hard work. I knew if I called an ambulance they'd come out with lights a blazing and wake everyone up, so I got Quentin a pillow and a blanket and told him I'd call for help in the morning. When I woke up a few hours later I heard him moaning and groaning.

I felt terrible when we finally got him to the hospital and learned that he'd broken seven ribs and punctured his lung. I didn't know he'd fallen against the stationary bike. Landing on the pedal is what did most of the damage.

He's been in so much pain, and I feel terrible about letting him lay on the floor for so long when he was hurting. I also feel bad for all the times I got mad at him. I know he hasn't wanted to be this way. I'm going to try really hard to be more patient and loving.

I'm very grateful that you're coming, although I don't anticipate this trip will be any fun for you. Quentin is not going to be happy about being moved into the nursing home in Inman, even though they offer excellent care there.

As I told you, it's very expensive, but I just can't take care of him in the shape he's in now. I don't know what I'll do if he doesn't die or get better in three months when the Medicare runs out. If he doesn't recover enough for me to take him home, I'll have to sell some land. If I do, I won't tell him. As you know, the land has always been sacred to the Kubin men.

There is a series of books about encounters people have had with angels. I've been reading a story to Quentin every night, and then we pray that his angel will come and help him make the transition. I believe he's ready.

It's late and I need to go to bed. I'll finish this in the morning.

July 17, 1999

Last night I was so tired I could barely put one foot in front of the other. I didn't think I'd have any trouble sleeping, but I did. I was thinking about Quentin. I was worrying about money. I was concerned about my own health and what was going to happen after the Medicare benefits run out.

Finally, after tossing and turning for a long time, I turned my worries over to God. I released everything to Him and I went into a deep, relaxed sleep. When I woke up I started receiving spiritual insights thick and fast. I got out of bed and wrote them down so I wouldn't forget. I wanted to share them with you so you will understand what I'm trying to do.

1. Do not fear any physical problem. Know that God will be with me helping me handle anything.

2. Live each day as it comes. Do not worry or project what might come in the future.

3. Do not set age limitations on my mental or physical abilities.

4. Realize that in God's eyes, life is eternal. He is the light of the world and will guide me.

Each morning ask God, "What are we going to do today?"

Lots of love,

Mom

Epilogue

I flew home a couple days after receiving Mom's last letter to help move Dad into the nursing home. We gathered a few possessions from home thinking he would enjoy being surrounded by familiar things. I'll never forget the look on his face when he pointed to a picture on the wall and said, "What's that doing here?"

When I explained that Mom couldn't take care of him any more his shoulders sagged and his chin fell to his chest. Later that evening I wheeled his chair into the dining room and took him to the table designated for people who needed assistance eating. I tried to act cheerful as I introduced him to three women already seated at the table. My voice and his presence didn't register with any of them. They all stared off into space. Their minds were gone. As soon as an aide came with Dad's food, I rushed out of the dining room, found a quiet corner and wept.

Later that night I participated in my parents' bedtime prayers. Mom did the talking, of course, and they held hands as she prayed for each of their kids, their grandchildren and great-grandchildren. Then Mom asked for Dad's angel to come and help him make the transition.

After we tucked Dad in, Mom and I returned to the

farm. Unable to sleep, I slipped out and went for a walk down the gravel road west of house. It was a road I'd walked many times in the past when I'd found myself in need of solace or a solution to a problem.

I heard the drone of an irrigation engine in a nearby field. Crickets chirped and frogs croaked as I walked and prayed. I begged God to take Dad. His suffering was terrible, and every day that he lived diminished Mom's health and stamina. I felt helpless and frustrated. I remembered how Alex and I had put our beloved dog down when she got ill, because we couldn't stand to watch her suffer. I was angry that getting out of this life had to be so hard for my dad, a good man, who didn't deserve this agony.

Into the dark I pleaded, "God, do something! Please stop his pain! End this! Help my mother! Let it be over!"

I don't know if that was the moment the fireflies appeared, or if I just hadn't noticed them until then, but suddenly there were thousands of little lights twinkling around me. They rose up out of the weeds in the ditches and flew in front of me as I walked. I was reminded of a Unity affirmation my mother had used since I was a child: "God goes before you and prepares the way." Suddenly I felt peaceful.

A few days later I bought an angel for Dad's room. When I gave it to him, he looked at me quizzically and said, "What's this?"

I wrapped my arms around him and said, "I wanted you to have an angel to help you make your transition."

He hugged me back and mumbled, "You're my angel."

I cried all the way to the airport. I was only home a few days when I got the call.

Although he'd slipped into a coma, Mom was certain he was aware that she had kissed him, told him she loved him and had given him permission to die. She was holding his hand when he took his last breath. It was July 27, 1999.

Initially she felt more relief than grief. He was no longer in pain. She wasn't going to have to sell the land to pay for his nursing care. She could finally get some rest.

I tried to convince her to move to Oregon, but my siblings were opposed. They felt the transition would have been too hard on her, and they were afraid they wouldn't see her any more. She wanted to move to an apartment in town, but Dad had asked her to wait a year before making any major changes.

So she stayed on the farm. She replaced the carpet and drapes and put up different wallpaper. For a few months she enjoyed her fresh new surroundings. When the initial elation wore off, she started to regret all the times she had gotten angry with Dad. She grieved over the fact that she hadn't called an ambulance the night he fell and broke his ribs, and she felt guilty over being so happy that he'd died before his Medicare ran out.

We talked on the phone often and I told her how much I admired her strength and patience. I told her over and over that she had absolutely no reason to feel guilty. Intellectually she agreed, but she struggled emotionally. She frequently woke up feeling Dad's presence in the bed. She said she could feel his warmth and the weight of his body next to hers. She said it was comforting, not spooky, but it bothered me. I convinced her to enroll in a grief counseling group at the church sponsored by Hospice. She did, and she quickly made friends and found comfort in their companionship.

She made a number of trips to Oregon, and the year after Dad died, Alex sent the two of us to Hawaii for a week to celebrate Mother's Day. She continued to read, study and pray. Her mind and spirit remained indomitable and her faith never wavered, but her body was worn out.

The summer following Dad's death, she was faced with another incredibly stressful situation. My brother Larry declared bankruptcy. Mom had cosigned a large note for him using the farm ground as collateral. So after all she'd gone through to preserve the land, it still had to be sold.

Alex and I went home to help move her out of the farmhouse and into an apartment in town. (If I had ever doubted my husband's love, I knew it went all the way to the bone when he wouldn't allow me to tackle that job alone.)

Mom was excited about her new apartment in a senior retirement building, and she loved her new social life. Unfortunately, it was short-lived. In the fall she started experiencing a series of TIA's – tiny strokes. In December, she had one that put her in the hospital. After a few days she was sent to a nursing home for rehabilitation. She was put in a room with an Alzheimer's patient. She told the doctors, nurses, and anyone else who would listen that SHE WAS NOT HAPPY.

I flew home just before Christmas and checked her out of the nursing home. She wanted a steak and a glass of wine, so we went to Applebee's – McPherson's newest and best restaurant.

Mom and Dad believed in angels, and after that night, I did too. Our server asked if we were celebrating a birthday or some other special occasion. I raised my wine in a toast to Mom and said, "No. We are just celebrating life and being together."

I have dined in a lot of fine restaurants, but I don't believe I've ever experienced more exquisite service than we did that night at Applebee's. After we finished our meal, that sweet young man brought us a huge slice of chocolate cake. He said it was his gift to us. It put us in a festive mood. After dinner we drove around town and looked at the Christmas lights.

I knew I might not have another chance, so I decided to tell my mother right then how important she had been in my life, how she had inspired me and kept me going through my darkest times, and how much I loved her. We held hands and laughed through our tears as we recalled shared memories.

Alex and I returned to Kansas once again in January. I massaged Mom's ankles and legs every night to try to increase her circulation, and we helped get her business affairs in order. She was slipping fast.

By late February I became increasingly concerned about her well-being. I knew she wasn't eating right, and I was afraid she wasn't taking her medication properly. I called my brother Greg in western Kansas and asked him to go check on her. I thought it was time for her to go into an assisted living facility.

Greg drove to McPherson that night, but when he arrived the building was locked and he couldn't get in. He called her from his motel and told her he would be there first thing in the morning. She was looking forward to seeing him.

The next morning Greg knocked on the door. When Mom didn't answer, he let himself in. He found her in the bathroom. The doctor said she was probably dead before she hit the floor. It was March 1, 2001 – just nineteen months after Dad's death.

When Greg called and told me the news I was both relieved and frightened. I was glad she had gotten out of this world with her dignity and independence intact. I was frightened because I couldn't imagine my life without her in it. She was my best friend, my confidant, and the "motherboard" of communication for our family. I felt empty knowing I would never again open my mailbox to find one of her fat, fantastic letters.

I'm happy she lived long enough to know Alex. When I told her I was dating him, the first thing she asked was, "How old is he?" When I told her, she said, "Go out. Have a nice dinner, but for God's sake don't marry him!" She changed her mind when she met him; and next to me, she became his greatest admirer. In 1993 neither one of us could have imagined how happy and full my life would become.

I'm also glad she lived long enough to know her prayers for her grandchildren were answered. Eric, Robert, and Annie survived the divorce, the job loss, the tumultuous teenage years, a variety of moves and other trials, to become self-sufficient, contributing members of society. They all live in Oregon. Two of Alex's children and their families also live close by. We treasure the opportunity to participate in all their lives and watch them grow personally and professionally.

I'm especially grateful that Madelyn was my mother. Being raised by her, I experienced the rare gift of unconditional love. Her thoughts and beliefs continue to have a profound impact on how I think and live my life.

In J.K. Rowling's book, *Chamber of Secrets*, Professor Dumbledore tells Harry Potter, "It is our choices, Harry, that show what we truly are, far more than our abilities."

Madelyn chose to believe in a loving and benevolent God who would give her the strength to face any physical, emotional, spiritual, or financial challenge. She chose to pick up the yoke when there was work to be done, to forgive thoughtless words and deeds, and to look for the good in everyone. And when she felt herself buckling under the weight of her burdens, she chose to change her attitude and view her difficulties as opportunities for growth.

Even though she's been gone a number of years, I still think of her nearly every day; and I continue to be influenced by her. I frequently smile when one of her little sayings pops to mind – such as: "Your Golden Years start the day your youngest child graduates from high school and end the day your health goes to hell."

Alex and I are in our "Golden Years" now, and we know it can all change in a heartbeat. I'm not afraid of death, but the process of getting there can be pretty scary. Even so, I am confident I will have the strength and faith to make the right choices and get through whatever lies ahead. After all, I am Madelyn Kubin's daughter.

2006 – Elaine and Alex's 10th wedding anniversary